Karma and Reincarnation

Contemporary Researches in Hindu Philosophy & Religion

(ISSN 0971-9628)

1. Idealistic Thought in Indian Philosophy; by Shuchita C. Divatia (ISBN 978-81-246-0021-4)
2. Karma and Reincarnation: The Vedāntic Perspective; by Muni Narayana Prasad (ISBN 978-81-246-0721-3)
3. Stonemill and Bhakti: From the Devotion of Peasant Women to the Philosophy of Swamies; by Guy Poitevin and Hema Rairkar (ISBN 978-81-246-0059-7)
4. Śaivism: Some Glimpses; by G.V. Tagare (ISBN 978-81-246-0076-4)
5. Advaita: A Conceptual Analysis; by A. Ramamurty (ISBN 978-81-246-0067-2)
6. Mind-Body Dualism: A Philosophic Investigation; by Alpana Chakraborty (ISBN 978-81-246-0071-9)
7. Hinduism and Scientific Quest; by T.R.R. Iyengar (ISBN 978-81-246-0077-1)
8. Indra and Other Vedic Deities — A Euhemeristic Study; by Uma Chakravarty (ISBN 978-81-246-0080-1)
9. Brahma-Vāda: Doctrine of Śrī Vallabhācārya; by G.V. Tagare (ISBN 978-81-246-0112-9)
10. The Science of Enlightenment: Enlightenment, Liberation and God — A Scientific Explanation; by Nitin Trasi (ISBN 978-81-246-0130-3)
11. Retrieving Sāṁkhya History: An Ascent from Dawn to Meridian; by Lallanji Gopal (ISBN 978-81-246-0143-3)
12. The Philosophical Foundations of Hinduism; by A. Ramamurty (ISBN 978-81-246-0163-1)
13. The Eternal Hinduism; by Baidyanath Saraswati (ISBN 978-81-246-0249-2)
14. Vedānta and its Philosophical Development; by A. Ramamurty (ISBN 978-81-246-0347-5)
15. Sāṁkhya-Yoga Epistemology; by Mukta Biswas (ISBN 978-81-246-0371-0)
16. A Sourcebook of Classical Hindu Thought; by Arvind Sharma (ISBN 978-81-246-0643-8)
17. A Treatise on Advaita Vedānta: English Translation of Vicāracandrodaya of Pandit Pitambara; by S. Bhuvaneshwari (ISBN 978-81-246-0707-7)

Contemporary Researches in Hindu Philosophy & Religion, no. 2

Karma and Reincarnation

Swami Muni Narayan Prasad

DK PRINTWORLD

Publishers of Indian Traditions

Cataloging in Publication Data — DK
[Courtesy: D.K. Agencies (P) Ltd. <docinfo@dkagencies.com>]

Narayana Prasad, *Muni,* 1938-
Karma and reincarnation / Swami Muni Narayan Prasad. — 2nd rev. ed.
p. cm. — (Contemporary researches in Hindu philosophy & religion ; no. 2)
Includes bibliographical references (p.) and index.
ISBN 13: 9788124607213

1. Karma. 2. Reincarnation — Hinduism. 3. Vedanta. I. Title. II. Series: Contemporary researches in Hindu philosophy & religion ; no. 2.

DDC 294.522 23

ISBN 13: 978-81-246-0721-3
First published in India in 1994
Reissued in 1995, 1999 and 2006
Second revised edition, 2014

Published and printed by:
D.K. Printworld (P) Ltd.
Regd. Office : *Vedaśrī,* F-395, Sudarshan Park
(Metro Station: Ramesh Nagar)
New Delhi–110 015
Phones : (011) 2545 3975; 2546 6019; *Fax* : (011) 2546 5926
e-mail : indology@dkprintworld.com
Web : www.dkprintworld.com

Preface to the Second Edition

THE book *Karma and Reincarnation* was reprinted three times since it was first published in 1994. Afterwards, the original book *Three Acharyas and Narayana Guru* of which this forms a chapter was thoroughly edited by my friend Ian Jaco Mathew of the United States. Then I thought it would be advisable to bring out the next edition of this book in the re-edited form which I feel is more readable to non-Indian minds. Matterwise, no change has been effected in this revised edition.

More and more inquisitive readers wanting to read the book make me feel the usefulness of the studies made to write it.

1 January 2014 **Muni Narayana Prasad**

Preface to the First Edition

THE Tao, through the unpredictably creative unfoldment of its infinite potential, gave me a chance to spend more than two years on the tiny island country of Fiji in the South Pacific. Reading and writing were my main engagements there beyond few classes which I gave every week.

In Fiji I used to give a class on *Bhagavad-Gītā* every Saturday evening. As I studied *Gītā* with the intention of teaching it, the overall philosophy of *Gītā* and the way it is developed chapter by chapter became somewhat clear to me. But the eighth chapter presented me with a stumbling block. I could not fit the reference to the two paths of the departed souls into the philosophy which is developed up to that point.

The class went on very well through the seventh chapter. But I hesitated to enter the next chapter because I did not want to teach something that was not clear to me. I postponed the class for a week. But the next Saturday also it was not clear what I should teach. Yet something within was prompting me to go on with the class. The class began with the usual prayer. While I was scanning through the beginning verses of the chapter after the prayer, to my great surprise it flashed into my mind that the answer to my doubt was in the third verse. The third and fourth verses discriminate what is imperishable from what is perishable. Birth and death are relevant only in the realm of the perishable. The Absolute Reality is not perishable; it is the imperishable *Brahman.* What is perishable is unreal. The question of death and the two paths of the departed souls are described in the section which deals with the world of perishables. The final teaching of *Gītā* does not pertain to what is unreal and perishable, but to what is real and imperishable. At the very end of the eighth chapter Śrī Kṛṣṇa tells Arjuna that a *yogī*'s mind will never be confounded by these twin paths. He recommends to Arjuna that he be a *yogī*. Slowly a clearer picture started coming into my view.

The third verse of eighth chapter also gives a precise definition of *karma*, perhaps the only definition of *karma* in all the scriptures of India. It makes it clear beyond all doubt that *karma* belongs to the imperishable Reality and not to any particular individual. The third chapter of *Gītā* further clarifies this idea when it says: "It is *prakṛti* (nature) according to its *guṇa*s (modalities) that does all *karma*s (actions)" and "only those who are deluded by their own ignorance think of themselves as the doers or agents of actions."

Prior to reaching Fiji, I had made a comparative study of the philosophies of Śaṅkara, Rāmānuja and Madhva as part of the "Introduction" to my extensive commentary on Narayana Guru's *Vedānta Sūtras.* One section of that was devoted to "Karma and Reincarnation". After the *Gītā* class on eighth chapter, I found that it had to be rewritten, because I found myself in a better position to make my original ideas clearer and more precise in the light of the new insights I had gained. After rewriting the whole chapter, I found it good enough to publish as an independent book.

All of us are born, live and die as part of nature. All the laws of nature are applicable to each of us without discrimination. One's birth and death happen according to these laws, whether one is a *jñānin* (enlightened person) or an *ajñānin* (ignorant person). If this is so, how can one go to one world through one path after departing, and another through another path to other worlds? Don't all people die according to the same laws of nature? Is it possible that there is one law for the *jñānin* and another for the *ajñānin*? Didn't both of them come into being from the same Reality or *Brahman,* according to Vedānta? Do they not go back to the same Reality, also according to Vedānta? How then can they have two different paths to two different worlds? All these problems had been puzzling me for a long time. The answers I found to these questions in Upaniṣads, *Bhagavad-Gītā* and the works of Narayana Guru are summarized in this small book. The absence of any mention of this topic in the works of Narayana Guru was the best guiding torch for me in the present study. In one sense, reincarnation is more a religious problem than a philosophical one. It is not based on any serious thinking, but merely on belief. It has thus become an article of faith in Eastern religions. This is perhaps the reason why Narayana Guru avoided this topic. The present study is an attempt to show how an Advaitin (non-dualist) looks at it.

The problem is an intriguing one which arises out of ignorance about one's own real existence. Therefore the final solution to the problem is to know the Reality. It is our hope that this study will help those people who wish to turn their attention towards knowing the Reality in themselves.

I am very grateful to Mrs Sheilah Johns of England who edited the manuscript of this book. Mr. Ian Jaco of America helped me re-editing the book to the present shape. The co-operation of the inmates of Narayana Gurukula at Varkala, such as Swami Mantra Chaitanya, Bro. Sudhakara Saukumarya, Reji Kumar, Sasidharan and Surendran also helped to make this book possible. My gratitude is beyond words to Messers D.K. Printworld of New Delhi for undertaking the responsibility of publishing this title. It is my hope that the entire commentary on Narayana Guru's *Vedānta Sūtras* may also be brought to the readers through them.

It is the kindly love and attention poured on me by Nataraja Guru in my younger days and later by Guru Nitya Chaitanya Yati that has made me bold enough to enter such fields of unanswered and unanswerable problems. I prostrate in front of them with great reverence before offering this to the readers.

Narayana Gurukula **Muni Narayana Prasad**
Varkala
5 May 1993

Contents

Introduction

REINCARNATION is a common belief among the religions of South Asian origin. This belief maintains the existence of a soul that successively takes up bodies some time after the death of each previous body. This belief further maintains that the nature of any succeeding birth depends on the nature of the soul's previous lives, especially in terms of its merits and demerits. But this belief has always been subject to widespread uncertainty and doubt. This is so despite the philosophical support given to it by great *ācārya*s, as well as being incessantly preached by all sorts of religious authorities. None the less, the belief in reincarnation is so deeply rooted in the Indian psyche that the findings of modern science have failed so far to overturn its popularity. Even in Buddhism, a religion that excludes the existence of a soul, this belief prevails as a basic tenet.

Karma and Reincarnation in Three Great Ācāryas' Teachings

IN THE ŚAṄKARA SYSTEM

Śaṅkara is well known as the propounder of non-dualism (Advaita). His stand on reincarnation actually remains ambiguous, despite all manner of explanations and elaborations given by his followers, as well as investigations done by generations of scholars. Doubtlessly, any concept of reincarnation implies admitting a multiplicity of souls, which, for Śaṅkara, can only be an illusory fabrication of *avidyā*. This stand must have obstructed any theory of reincarnation from being admitted into the doctrinal core of Advaita Vedānta.

All effects of *avidyā*, by necessity, should be considered unreal; hence as effects of *avidyā*, the multiplicity of souls must be unreal, along with birth, death and rebirth. Since Vedānta's sole aim is to rid oneself of *avidyā* and its effects, such notions can never form part of its core teaching, nor reflect the nature of Reality Itself. Their unreality, it is to be admitted, dawns only for a *jñānī*; yet this, in no way makes an *ajñānī*'s wrong conception of life any more real. This may have been the reason why Śaṅkara does not treat the topic directly in works like *Vivekacūḍāmaṇi*, whereas he takes pains to explain the notion in his commentaries on *Brahma-Sūtras* and Upaniṣads.

It should be remembered that all citations in *Brahma-Sūtras* have Upaniṣads as their source. And what the Upaniṣadic *ṛṣis*' original visions and intentions were remain unclear. Here we find no definitive theory of reincarnation.

But in his original works, or at least the ones attributed to him, Śaṅkara does elaborate upon the concept of *karma* and its residues. In the following verses of *Vivekacūḍāmaṇi* he says:

> *Sañcita* (accumulated *karmas* of the past) and *āgāmī* (future *karmas*) are destroyed by the fire of wisdom. *Prārabdha* (*karma* already begun but not yet fruitioned) indeed is very powerful; its exhaustion in the wise is by their cheerful endurance. —v. 453
>
> As long as one's identity is with body, alone is *prārabdha* relevant (*prārabdhaḥ siddhyati tadā yadā dehātmanā sthitiḥ*). —v. 460

In other words, *prārabdha* only appears meaningful in the state of ignorance. Furthermore, there are two more kinds of *karma*. Śaṅkara emphatically says:

> If the effects of ignorance are completely destroyed by wisdom, how can the present body exist? Only intending to clear up this doubt of the ignorant do the scriptures speak of *prārabdha* from a superficial point of view, but not intending to teach that body continues to be real for the attainers of wisdom. — vv. 462-63

The body and other conditioning factors (*upādhis*) are but superimpositions upon the unborn and deathless *Ātman*. It is by these ignorance-caused superimpositions that one mistakenly identifies oneself with the body. This in turn results in the notion that one has *karmas* along with their residues, as well as notions of birth, death and rebirth. Therefore, the notion that the self takes rebirth after death is an affect of *avidyā*. Śaṅkara again says:

> How can the superimposed be real?
> How can the unreal have birth?
> How can the unborn have death?
> How can the unreal have *prārabdha*?
>
> —v. 461

Such is the significance of birth, death and rebirth in the light of Advaita. Though philosophers and religious authorities, including Advaitins, have long supported the idea of rebirth, we feel it is vital to reinvestigate and reconsider what *ṛṣis* really meant by the term "rebirth" as found in the scriptures.

IN THE RĀMĀNUJA SYSTEM

Rāmānuja was the great *ācārya* or master who originated the school of Vedānta known as Viśiṣṭādvaita (qualified non-dualism). His basic tenet was that souls are many and eternal. Rāmānuja conceives of souls, together with inert matter, as forming the body of *Brahman*, which he prefers to call Nārāyaṇa. These souls, both bound and liberated, retain their individuality. Therefore, statements made by *Bṛhadāraṇyaka Upaniṣad*, to the effect that souls travel to the world of *Brahman* or to the world of the moon, are taken quite literally. After death, Rāmānuja conceives of souls travelling one of two possible paths. Upon reaching the world of Nārāyaṇa, liberated souls enjoy eternal service before Nārāyaṇa, from where they return not. Conversely, bound souls reach the world of *pitṛs* (the souls of ancestors), wherefrom they will afterwards return to this earthly world in accordance with their *karmas*. When commenting on *sūtra* 3.1.8 of *Brahma-Sūtras* and quoting an Upaniṣad for authoritative support, Rāmānuja says:

> The scriptural text is: "Those whose conduct has been good" (V.10.7), which means that among the souls that have returned, those whose *karma* is good obtain a good birth as brāhmaṇas or the like, while those whose *karma* is bad are born again as low creatures — dogs, pigs, *cāṇḍāla*s and the like.

In support of this contention, Rāmānuja profusely quotes the *Gautama-Dharma-Sūtras* and *Āpastamba-Sūtras*, though neither is a basic scripture. A passage quoted from the former says:

> Men of the several castes and . . . , who always stand firm in the works prescribed for them, enjoy after their death the rewards of their works, and by virtue of a remnant (of their works) they are born again in excellent countries, castes and families, endowed with beauty, long life, learning in the Vedas, wealth, good conduct, happiness and wisdom. Those who act in the contrary manner perish.

Rāmānuja describes the kinds of *karma* that adhere to a doer as follows:

> Nor is it possible for works, the fruits of which have not yet been enjoyed, and those the result of which has not been wiped out by expiatory ceremonies, should be destroyed by the enjoyment of the fruits of other works. Hence those who have gone to that world return with a remnant of their work.

Rāmānuja relies mainly on secondary scriptural evidences to maintain this theory. This is possible for Rāmānuja because scriptures have authority by virtue of the people's faith, not rational thought. So like Śaṅkara, Rāmānuja chiefly relies on scriptures to validate his own stands. Yet when countering opponents, like Śaṅkara, he still relies primarily on logical reasoning as Śaṅkara did, with some exceptions.

For Rāmānuja, the tenet of rebirth concerns the future of departing souls. It also means that the future of the world is endless. His theory maintains that the peculiar characteristics and *karmas* of souls, *in toto*, do not die at the dissolution of the world. They merely shrink and then endure within the inseparable subtleties of Nārāyaṇa. After lying in wait, they expand again into more definite forms during the next Creation.

IN THE MADHVA SYSTEM

For Madhva, whose system of thought is known as dualism (Dvaita Vedānta), souls are seen to be many, varied and eternal, though dependent. As such, the reincarnation of souls is naturally taken for granted. So then, the images of life after death portrayed in *Bṛhadāraṇyaka* and *Chāndogya* Upaniṣads are to be interpreted literally.

Yet the Madhva system stands apart from the others in one respect. Characteristics peculiar to each individual do not depend on past *karmas* alone. Each individual reacts to a given situation in a way that is peculiar to that individual. Previously acquired *karmas* alone cannot explain the varied nature of present *karmas*. They vary because individual souls are innately different and Madhva calls these differences *svarūpa-bheda*. These innate differences manifest as differences in the distinctive character or temperament of each individual.

Differing from Rāmānuja, Madhva maintains that God's act of creating and destroying the world is an incessant process. It is not merely an event preceding or succeeding the Great Deluge. In this context, repeated birth is counted a kindly boon that helps souls liberate themselves from the heavy burden of *karmas*, and partaking in the fruits of their *karmas* will help them towards this end.

NARAYANA GURU

Narayana Guru was a *ṛṣi* who revalued and restated Vedānta in the twentieth century. Even though questions of life after death and reincarnation hold an important place in the Vedāntic schools of thought, it is conspicuously absent in his philosophy. The reason for this glaring omission could be ascribed to the fact that such a problem pertains to realm of the unreal and is therefore but a relic of *avidyā*.

Now we will delve deep into this issue, commencing with its origin in Vedic lore and proceeding unto its non-appearance in the philosophy of Narayana Guru in modern times.

1

Vedic References

To the critically-minded Indians of yore, a doctrine was considered acceptable only if it concurred with three tests, namely scriptural evidence (*śruti*), reasonableness (*yukti*) and actual experience (*anubhava*). Undoubtedly, the present problem concerns something no one has ever actually experienced. The means used for the third test — *anubhava* — thus will not work in the present case. Reasoning too is ultimately based on actual experience. No reasoning is possible without the experiences of actual life. Thus the second test, dependent on the third test, also fails in the present case. The only remaining source of knowledge, then, is scriptural evidence. The acceptance or non-acceptance of any scriptural teaching about something, which can never be verified in actual life, is merely a matter of belief. In short, the topic we are dealing with is such that its inherent inconclusiveness can never be eliminated.

Vedic literature is the only source material available to aid us in studying the variety of ideas regarding the hereafter, as well as how the idea of reincarnation took root in common man's mind. Historians have found ample evidence to indicate the prevalence of the belief in life after death, even in the pre-Vedic culture of India. There was a practice of encasing dead infants within womb-like earthen pots, and then burying them inside their houses or in their proximity. According to historians, this practice had behind it the belief that a dead child would come back into a new body born of the same family.

However it may be, it is certain that, whether among primitives or the civilized, inquisitiveness about what happens after death is common and natural. Man's irresistible quest to attain immortality is equally universal and natural. In one sense we could say that immortality is assured through procreation. It is one's own self that continues through one's offspring. In another sense, we could say that those who have attained the higher realms of knowledge realize immortality by visualizing the immortal Reality (*ātman*) as enduring in and through all transient visible forms. It is not our aim here to judge the validity of these two kinds of immortality. Rather we would like to see for ourselves at what level of understanding or to what extent these two different concepts become relevant.

A.B. Keith in *The Religion and Philosophy of the Veda and the Upaniṣads* makes a study pursuing the Vedic concept of the soul and its state after death, as well as the role *karma* plays in this process. This well-researched study indicates that no clear or definitive conception of life after death exists in the Vedas. His study rather illustrates the unavoidable uncertainty inherent in the whole subject. So just as in modern times, these early ancients also could give no clear answer to the question of life after death. Even upon becoming convinced of this unavoidable uncertainty, one still may ask, "Why should it be unclear?" Such a protest is natural enough, because our human minds seem conditioned by the preconception that something is convincing only when everything about it can be explained down to the last detail. This conditioning conduces us to ask such questions. But there is a convenient way to put an end to such unanswerable questions. That is, tell a story that sounds both supernatural and definitive. This way was used profusely by *ṛṣis* of ages gone by. It is not difficult to presume that such differing stories narrated in the Vedas, Upaniṣads, Purāṇas and Itihāsas eventually came to pass for religious dogmas in the minds of people only able or willing to believe a detailed or colourful explanation, rather than give the matter careful consideration.

Let us now examine the Vedic concept of reincarnation and *karma*. Keith points out two types of passages dealing with these in the Vedas when saying:

> On the one hand there have been direct references to metempsychosis in *Ṛgveda*, and on the other there have been traces of these ideas which explain the genesis of the conception.[1]

He further says:

> The references to transmigration, which have been in *Ṛgveda*, are all of the most improbable character, it is to ignore the nature of poetry to press the wish that there may be long life for man among the gods into the view that it contemplates rebirth: the attempt to find references to it in two of the verses of the riddle hymn of Dīrghatamas is bold but not very plausible. The allusion, in which Vasiṣṭha is made to refer to his previous birth, is quite impossible and the same criticism can be applied to every other case.[2]

The following passage of *Ṛgveda* is one that supposedly supports the theory of reincarnation:

> Take your seat, O Yama, on the sacred grass, together with the priests of old and with *pitṛ*s. — *ṚV* X.14.4

The word *pitṛ*, literally "father", means "the departed". It does not specifically mean the soul of the departed. Even if it has such a connotation, this passage does not give the least hint of reincarnation of souls.

Another stanza, commonly taken to be an immediate reference to reincarnation, is found in the Dīrghatamas Sūkta of *Ṛgveda*. It reads:

> That which has death and that which is deathless have the same

---

1 A.B. Keith, *The Religion and Philosophy of the Veda and the Upaniṣads*, Delhi: Motilal Banarsidass, 1970, p. 570.

2 Ibid., pp. 570-71.

> source. Possessed by the desire for enjoying food, together they go downwards and upwards. Thus they exist eternally in this world moving around. The one is always known and the other remains unknown.[3]

The theory of reincarnation and the related one of *karma* is attributed to this stanza, when interpreted by adding the phrase, "as a result of doing evil deeds" after "they go downwards" and "in order to enjoy the fruits of one's own actions" after "moving around". But when no such words are inserted, this passage does not suggest any idea of reincarnation. This peculiarity of using interpolation can be seen in most cases where scholars quote scriptural evidences to support the idea of reincarnation, or to see the idea within the context of the scriptures.

In the Vedic passage cited above, we prefer to consider "that which has death" as standing for the visible and perishable aspect of existence, and "that which is deathless" for the imperishable and invisible aspect of existence. If it were supposed the passage refers to the state after death, then the words, "together they go downwards and upwards" would have no reason to appear. If it were assumed there was such a movement of the soul, then it must be done without a body. But that is not what is said in this passage. Evidently, therefore, the movement upwards and downwards is not of the soul after death. Above all, the said movement takes place when one is possessed by the desire for enjoying food. We prefer to consider food here as standing for all that is valued and enjoyed in life. This makes it clear then that the movement downwards and upwards is in a world of values, or concerns what is dear to one in life. Everyone has a value-world of their own in which they live. What is dear to one in life depends on this value-world. Whereas one person may consider money as the highest value in life, another leaves that value behind to seek a world of knowledge that he considers

---

3 *Ṛgveda* I.64.38.

the highest value. Those who treat higher values dearly are frequently and poetically portrayed as going upward. Naturally those who conversely treat the lowest values dearly are portrayed going downward. So we can understand the stanza afresh by seeing that it pertains to the world of here and now. This movement in the value-world could have been mistaken for the movement of souls after death because this stanza refers to the mortal and immortal. But the immortal need not necessarily mean the soul, or the mortal mean the body. The stanza only says that these two have the same source and they exist always together. This could be better understood in a metaphysical sense, where life can be considered the meeting place of the immortal and mortal aspects of one and the same Reality. Such is the nature of the few Vedic passages supposedly in direct support of the belief in reincarnation.

The Vedic passages, which possibly suggest the belief in life after death, also deserve consideration. Suggestive Vedic ideas adduced by Oldenberg are: that birds are forms assumed by the Fathers (ancestors); and that the Fathers creep about the roots of the plants; and that the practice of alighting of an insect or some animal on an outspread garment will serve as proxy for missing mortal remains when invoking the soul of a deceased.[4] In stanza X.16.3 of *Ṛgveda*, we find a reference that says going to heaven or earth accords with one's merits. It reads:

> May your eyes go to the sun,
> May your self (breath) go to air,
> May you go either to heaven or earth
> According to your merits;
> Or even the middle world;
> It is there you find what is good for you;
> Find your place among the vegetables
> Along with the bodily limbs.

---

4 Keith, op. cit., p. 571.

It is presumed that transmigration of the soul is suggested by the words, "May you go to earth". Keith points out:

> . . . the importance of transmigration lies precisely in the fact that the doctrine is an ethical system. . . . That it should have been so fully accepted by the people in course of time was doubtless aided by such views as that mentioned. But no such view could create metempsychosis as a system of the marked character of the Indian view.[5]

---

[5] Keith, op. cit., pp. 571-72.

2

Ārtabhāga's Doubt and the Mystery of Karma

In *Śatapatha Brāhmaṇa* (I.5.3-4) we can find indirect suggestions alluding to the idea of reincarnation. More direct references can be found in *Bṛhadāraṇyaka* and *Chāndogya* Upaniṣads. In the well-known section of the former called "Yājñavalkīya", we see an expanded version of the citation we examined in X.16.3 of *Ṛgveda*.

Jāratkārava Ārtabhāga ends his own questioning of Yājñavalkya's understanding of *Brahman* by asking:

> Yājñavalkya, when the voice of a dead man goes to fire, his breath to the wind, his eye to the sun, his mind to the moon, his hearing into the quarters of heaven, his body into the earth, his soul into space, the hairs of his head into plants, the hairs of his body into trees and his blood and semen are placed in water, what then becomes of his person (*puruṣa*)?
>
> Ārtabhāga, my dear, take my hand. We two only will know of this. This is not for us to speak of in public.
>
> The two went away and deliberated. What they said was *karma*. What they praised was *karma*. Verily, one becomes good by good action, bad by bad action.
>
> Thereupon Jāratkārava Ārtabhāga held his peace.[1]

To see a suggestion of metempsychosis in relation to *karma* here,

1 *Bṛhadāraṇyaka Upaniṣad* III.ii.13.

one must implant those concepts into the text while interpreting. Śaṅkara interprets this verse to concern the death of the ignorant, and the previous two verses to concern the state after death of a liberated person. But we see no indication in these stanzas to warrant such a division. All three stanzas here only refer to the dying person as "such a person" (*ayam puruṣaḥ*). The stanza previous to these three evidently concerns a deity that makes death his food. It reads as follows:

> Yājñavalkya, said he (Ārtabhāga), since everything here is food for death, what pray is that divinity for whom death is food?
>
> Fire, verily is death. It is the food of water. He (who knows this) overcomes death.[2]

The "everything here" of this passage has been described in the preceding nine stanzas. They consist of the senses and their objects, termed as perceivers (*graha*s) and over-perceivers (*atigraha*s). All these become food for death. Then who is it that has death for his food? This is the question here asked by Ārtabhāga.

To answer, Yājñavalkya first compares death to fire, the all-consuming element. Fire is then said to become food for water. Thus there should be something standing for water that makes the fire death its food. This water must be *Brahman*. Those who know *Brahman* overcome death. Such is the teaching of the present passage in the Upaniṣad. The two stanzas that Śaṅkara interprets as the death of a liberated person are sequels to this section. These stanzas run as follows:

> "Yājñavalkya", said he, "when such a person dies, do the vital breaths move up from him or do they not?"
>
> "No", said Yājñavalkya, "they are gathered together right here. He (the body) swells up, inflated the man (body) lies."

---

2 *Bṛhadāraṇyaka Upaniṣad* III.ii.10.

> "Yājñavalkya", said he, "when such a person dies, what is it that does not leave him?"
>
> "The name. The name is infinite, and infinite are the Viśve-devas (All-gods). Thereby he (who knows this) wins an infinite world."[3]

The stanza quoted first, which praises *karma*, is a continuation of these stanzas. This stanza also refers to the same "such a person". Therefore it seems more cogent to take the person referred to in these sequential stanzas to be one and the same. These stanzas, with no interpolation, do not give even a remote suggestion to think otherwise. So this sequence of stanzas may well connote an entirely different sense than is commonly interpreted.

As we have seen, the stanzas preceding these three teach that death is the fire that consumes all the constituent elements of an individual being, and *Brahman* is the fire that consumes death. The person referred to here evidently stands for an individual being. The individual being is food for death and death is food for *Brahman*. Such is the scheme of life in which the multiplicity of individual beings and the unity of the ultimate Reality have their non-difference. Here, death is, as it were, a connecting link between the perishable living beings and the imperishable Existence. Birth then is the obverse channel that forms the same link. The life of a person, the life of each of us, has to be seen as forming part of such a total scheme. It is only in such a scheme, which correlates everything together, that the questions such as, "what happens to the vital breath (*prāṇa*) on death?" and "what would not leave him after death?" become pertinent. When Yājñavalkya answers these questions, he simply says, "the vital breaths are gathered up right here". This means, it simply becomes unified with the total scheme of life in which air plays a major role. That which does not leave him is name alone.

---

3 *Bṛhadāraṇyaka Upaniṣad*, III.ii.11-12.

It was stated in stanza 10 that everything here would become food for death. Yet there is another divinity (*devatā*) that consumes even death. The word *devatā* etymologically means "that which is of the essence of effulgence". In the Upaniṣadic context, all the divinities stand for some form of functional consciousness. The essence of consciousness, we know, is nothing but an experience of brightness.

Death is the fire that consumes everything. The only element that can consume fire is water. Hence the Reality beyond death, that bestows death so as to ensure the continuity and novelty of life, is compared to water. All phenomenal appearances in life such as birth, sustenance and death have to be intuitively visualized as the emerging and remerging of waves on the surface of *Brahman*'s great waters. Such is the teaching of the stanza quoted above.

Stanza 11 depicts what happens to the transient aspects of the individual being upon death. The vital breaths, which find their oneness right here with the total atmosphere, as well as the body which swells up, both stand for the transient subtle and gross aspects of personal existence. The next stanza considers the eternal aspects. Yājñavalkya replies that only name will remain of the person. This needn't be taken as pertaining to actual name of the person alone. What is eternal in any individuated entity can never be seen objectively. Yet everyone knows something eternal exists. Thus we name the eternal Reality according to how we are capable of conceiving of it. *Ātmā*, *Brahman*, Tao, Yahweh, God, Allah and the like are such names. Thus the name becomes as eternal and endless as the Reality it denotes, as suggested in the passage.

Viśve-devas (All-gods) are endless in the same sense. They are mythological symbols for all the functional modulations of consciousness together. Whatever form consciousness functionally manifests itself as, it does not become different from that consciousness in essence. The same is so with the ultimate Reality. Whatever be the form in which it individuates itself, it does not become different from that Reality, just as whatever ornament-form that gold assumes, it does not become different from gold. The final teaching of all the Upaniṣads is that this ultimate Reality is nothing but pure Consciousness (*cit*). Such is the implication of the words "All-gods are endless".

The stanza that praises *karma* is sequel to this and has to be understood as such. These stanzas are not meant to be understood disjunctively. The vital breaths and the body mentioned in stanza 11 and the name and All-gods of stanza 12 have to be seen as non-different from the water of *Brahman* in stanza 10. We can see then that stanza 13 is a summary of the deliberation begun at the very start of this section.

The reference in the said passage to the voice of the dead man going to fire, breath to wind, eyes to the sun, mind to the moon, etc. is usually interpreted as all the senses going to their concerned presiding deities. This stanza is commonly treated as concerning the death of an ignorant man. But the very same concept of the presiding deity (*devatā*) could be intuitively understood in a more philosophic sense without considering it as referring to the death of an ignorant person.

Traditionally in Vedānta, every aspect of an individual has a corresponding aspect in the universal context, and these two are always to be seen as counterparts, like the head and tail sides of a coin. Even the individual person (*puruṣa*) has a counterpart called *virāṭ-puruṣa* (the cosmic person). In this context, every aspect in the individual person has a corresponding aspect in the cosmic person. This is not to be understood in the literal sense. This is only a poetically conceived, methodological device employed to emphasize that these two aspects are not to be understood disjunctively in any context, but to belong to a total scheme. A detailed picture of such a scheme could be seen in the first chapter of *Aitareya Upaniṣad*. According to this scheme, the eyes of the individual have the sun for their counterpart in the cosmic person. Similarly, vital breath has air, body has earth, mind has moon, ears have the four quarters, words have fire, hairs of the head have plants, hairs of the body have trees, semen has water and so on.

By the event of death, all the aspects that sustained the individual as an entity merge with the corresponding universal aspects, rendering them indistinct. But even before death a person is in a state of oneness with the totality, only appearing as a distinct form. This is the only difference between the two states. Nothing goes anywhere. The merger of the distinct forms into their own indistinct totality serves also as an impetus for the emergence of new forms by an intrinsic law of its own. For example, a dead body buried becomes manure for plants and trees. This intrinsic law or vital force that ensures the continuity of the world is to be called *karma*. We'll have more to say about this later. Nowhere is it claimed that a newly-emerged form is the same individual that had merged and re-merged prior to it. The factors that constitute an individual do not proceed directly to a new individual. Instead, they merge with the totality from which new forms then emerge. Such is the grand flux of Nature. The "paths" that souls take after death, as described in some scriptures, could be understood as descriptions of this same scientifically unitive vision of life. We shall examine these "paths" later.

The essence of Ārtabhāga's question in this passage could be said to be this: what becomes of a person upon death when all the individual's specific life functions merge with their corresponding cosmic ones?

Death is an occurrence by which all specific attributes of an individual disappear. It is not a process of becoming nothing.

What really exists cannot become non-existent. The previous stanza stated that only name would not leave the person. So the present question seeks for an answer beyond the realm of names or words. Yājñavalkya hesitates to answer this question in public. Then he takes the hand of Ārtabhāga and tells him, "this is not to be discussed in public." So they go outside the hall and discuss the matter privately. It is to be surmised from the silent climax of this dramatic situation that there is a mysterious element in it that would not be understood and appreciated by ordinary listeners. This mysterious element is something beyond words as suggested in a prior verse. A real *guru* communicates this part of the teaching only to a fully competent disciple who has established an intimate bipolar relationship (*pārasparya*) with him. Others would not understand it and would even ridicule it. When this secret is fully understood by a disciple, all his doubts vanish and he becomes fully satisfied in having attained what he was searching for. That must be why Ārtabhāga held his peace after their private dialogue. But what renders this dramatic scene of the Upaniṣad all the more mysterious is that it does not reveal what they privately spoke of. Śaṅkara, as well as any reader, can only guess what was going on between them. Yet it ended with Ārtabhāga coming to silence and satisfaction.

The only indication regarding the topic discussed is that it was about *karma* and what they praised was *karma*. Before we examine the implications of *karma* we have to be aware of the oneness of the individual and cosmic forms of existence. When all the conditioning factors that distinguish one individual from another merge with their counterparts in the cosmic aspect, what remains would be a non-duality where both the individuated and cosmic aspects are meaningless. If we think in terms of the broader meaning of *puruṣa*, when the perishable person (*kṣara-puruṣa*) merges with the imperishable person (*akṣara-puruṣa*), what remains would be the non-dual Supreme Person (*puruṣottama*), to use the terminology of *Bhagavad-Gītā*, chapter XV. To say that such a Supreme Person exists, would be as valid as it would be invalid, because it is merely a play with words or names. It was stated in the immediately preceding stanza that only name remains of a person who dies. There is a secret in this, which would not be understood and appreciated by ordinary listeners. Therefore they conversed in secret. But it is not made clear what that mysterious *karma* is and whose it is. Was it the *karma* of the person who died? Or is it of the cosmic person in whom he merged? It is not clear. This uncertainty is not a justification for concluding that the Upaniṣad supports the theory of reincarnation. For those whose minds are already conditioned by a belief in such a concept, this stanza might seem to support their belief. But without first determining whose *karma* it is, it would be impossible to determine whether this section of the Upaniṣad supports the idea of reincarnation. We should probe deeply whether or not such an idea or theory was even in the mind of Yājñavalkya.

3

What Is Karma and Who Does It?

THE *Bṛhadāraṇyaka Upaniṣad* helps us decide the nature of *karma* (action), as discussed between Yājñavalkya and Ārtabhāga, by giving a hint; namely, they praised it. In some contexts, *karma* refers to an individual's actions. The actions of an individual, we know, need not always be praiseworthy. Even if they were praiseworthy, it would be based on some relativistic considerations prevailing in the society. It will never be the praiseworthiness of an absolutist nature. *Karma* can also be understood in the sense of Vedic ritualism. Such rituals are apparently not considered praiseworthy by the Upaniṣads. *Bhagavad-Gītā* is the only Indian scripture that examines *karma*, as acceptable to Vedānta, touching all its aspects, which in one place says, "the way of *karma* is elusively subtle indeed" (IV.17).

It should be determined from the very outset, who it is that possesses *karma* deliberated on by Yājñavalkya and Ārtabhāga. We are familiar with actions such as thinking, speaking and numerous bodily actions. Is the capability to perform these actions our own making? No, all these occur as part of the totality of Nature. They naturally happen even as water flows, fire burns and trees grow. Each one of us is endowed with certain capabilities as part of the creative urge of the total Nature. Even the powers of knowledge and volition to make use of these capabilities, as situations demand, are in us as part of that very same creative urge of Nature. Neither is our free will, of our own free making. It is Nature that functions in all these. Upon reflection, we come to realize that it is not we who then do actions, but that all actions are done by Nature. Nature is called *prakṛti* in Sanskrit, which means, "that which does everything properly" (*prakarṣeṇa-karoti-iti-prakṛtiḥ*). That means, *prakṛti* cannot be *prakṛti* without action (*kṛti* or *karma*).

Bhagavad-Gītā brings this into unequivocal relief by saying:

> Irrespective of the occasion, it is Nature that through *guṇa*s (three Nature-modalities) accomplishes every act. One stupefied by the "I"-sense, however, thinks oneself as the actor.[1]

An action should have an actor (*kartā*). That means, there may be someone to claim, "I am doing this." On earth, it is probably only humankind who has this definite sense of agency, though all living beings are naturally active. Like everything and every being, the human is born as part of Nature and lives as part of Nature. But people usually do not realize themselves as an integral part of Nature, and therefore are oblivious to the fact that their abilities of knowing, volition and doing works are merely part of the creative function of Nature. Because of this obliviousness, people consider themselves the doers of all such actions. Such a person is called *vimūḍhātmā* (the stupefied one or the stupid). Only such stupefied ones think with a sense of agency, and in that sense they alone have *karma*. But those who see themselves, along with the variety of actions they perform, as integral parts of Nature, even while engaged in those actions, do not consider themselves the actors or possessors of *karma*, and so they do not have *karma*. They know it is Nature that functions through them in a particular way; hence *karma* does not bind them. Thus, *Gītā*'s basic stand regarding *karma* is that if there is *karma*, it is Nature that has it. And in the case of Nature, it has no sense of agency, so there is no question of *karma* for Nature either.

---

1 *Bhagavad-Gītā* III.27.

This is also made clear in *Gītā* thus:

> Neither *kartr̥tva* (doership) nor *karma*s (actions) themselves is disposed by the Lord among beings of the world, nor is the doer's union with the fruits of *karma*s allocated. What works out here is simply the creative becoming of the Self.[2]

Here the Lord (*prabhuḥ*) signifies *Brahman* or the Absolute. *Brahman* is not an inert entity. It is dynamic and creative in and of Itself. That which is dynamic is always in a state of change. When one state changes into another, it is considered an event. At every event there is an action or function occurring that causes a transformation. Every such transformation that takes place could be considered a *karma*. Where does it take place? It is in the total Nature. As such, no individual performs actions. It is merely a spontaneous transformation that takes place in Nature. *Karma* discussed in the above *Gītā* verse as "the creative becoming of the Self (*svabhāvaḥ*)", is to be understood in this light.

Gītā is the only Indian scripture that defines *karma* precisely and scientifically. The definition reads:

> That specific creative urge (*visargaḥ*) which causes the emergence of all existent beings is designated *karma*.[3]

This definition comes as the second half of a verse. In its first half we see that this *karma* belongs to the imperishable *Brahman*. Even the chapter is named *Akṣara-Brahma-Yoga* (The Yoga of the Imperishable Brahman). The first line of that verse equates the imperishable with *Brahman* when it says, "The imperishable is *Brahman* the Supreme" (*akṣaram brahma paramam*). Every individual entity, uniquely configured as the result of the unfoldment of the inner creative urge in the imperishable *Brahman*, is called *adhyātma* (*svabhāvo 'dhyātmam ucyate*). The word *adhyātma* in the Upaniṣadic

---

2 *Bhagavad-Gītā* V.14.

3 Ibid. VIII.3: *bhūta-bhāvodbhava-karo visargaḥ karma saṁjñitaḥ.*

context does not mean "spiritual" as is understood in ordinary literature. It means that which makes one's own individuated existence (*ātmā*) the basis (*adhi*) of enquiry. Each individual entity is the expression of the inner nature (*svabhāvaḥ*) of *Brahman*. The process of this creative unfoldment or self-expression is called *karma*. *Brahman*, in this process of self-unfoldment or self-expression, is called *prakṛti*. *Prakṛti* is the causal force (*śakti*) for all the phenomenal becoming. *Gītā* emphasizes this point when it says:

> By virtue of my *prakṛti*, I emanate again and again the whole aggregate of beings, subject as they are to the necessary compulsion of *prakṛti*.[4]

Śrī-Kṛṣṇa, representing the Absolute, concedes that He Himself is the one who does all *karmas*. He then washes His hands clean of any sense of agency in doing those actions. *Brahman* is always indifferent and unattached to all these actions, as is stated in the very next verse. Again we read in verse 10:

> By Me presiding, *prakṛti* gives birth to both the movable and immovable entities; because of this, O Arjuna, this changeful world revolves.[5]

Narayana Guru confirms this when he says:

> The Self alone, through *māyā*, does actions, by assuming numerous forms.[6]

The Self understood by Narayana Guru and the "Me" of *Bhagavad-Gītā* are not two. An individual, his knowledge, his free will, his actions, all form merely a spark in the beginningless, endless and inexhaustible creative urge of the imperishable Causal Reality. To become truly aware of this is to attain non-duality through action. This is the *karma-yoga* taught in *Gītā*. What we name birth,

---

4 *Bhagavad-Gītā*, IX.8.

5 Ibid., IX.10.

6 Narayana Guru, *Darśana-Mālā* (Garland of Visions) VI.1.

life and death are only the emergence, existence and re-merging of the small ripples from the surface of an endless ocean. That endless ocean is the Causal Reality, and all such events happen as the result of its own *karma*. This Causal Reality is Consciousness in essence. Because it is often poetically compared to an ocean, it is called *saṁvit-sāgara* (the Ocean of Consciousness).

Narayana Guru in his *Ātmopadeśa-Śatakam* paints a vivid picture of life *in toto* as driven by the force of *karma*. It reads as follows:

> Like waves arising in the ocean,
> Bodies one by one arise and then merge again;
> Alas! Where is an end to this?
> It is the endless *karma* going on
> In the ocean of primal Consciousness.[7]

This *karma*, always mysterious, is praiseworthy. It must be the *karma*, in this mysterious sense, that was praised by Yājñavalkya and Ārtabhāga in their dialogue held in private.

The purport of Ārtabhāga's last question to Yājñavalkya, and their ensuing private dialogue, could be taken as follows:

What becomes of a person when all his individuating factors merge with their corresponding cosmic factors?

The specific and universal forms are merely two different conditioned aspects of one and the same unconditioned Reality. Thus when all specifying factors become one with the corresponding universal ones, what remains would be the unconditioned Reality, which is neither specific nor universal. This non-dual Reality could be called *puruṣottama*, using the terminology of *Gītā*. This *puruṣottama* transcends both the perishable person and the imperishable person. This Supreme

---

7 Narayana Guru, *Ātmopadeśa-Śatakam* (One Hundred Verses of Self-Instruction) v. 56.

Person is pure Consciousness in essence and It expresses Itself through Its own innate creative urge. This creative Reality has nothing else to sustain Itself. It exists by Itself, in Itself, for Itself. This creative urge is the pure action (*karma*) as defined by *Gītā*. It is not the *karma* of anyone. Hence the only possible answer to the question asked by Ārtabhāga would be somewhat like this:

What remains would be the one ultimate Reality and Its pure creative urge or *karma*. It is this creative urge that makes the phenomenal world appear and revolve cyclically in the same Reality. Yājñavalkya was teaching, one would presume, this secret of *karma* to Ārtabhāga privately. (Our words.)

The non-dual Reality and its creative urge are related not as a substance and its attribute. Rather the very essence of Reality is the creative urge. There is evidently a mystery lurking at the core of this, which would become unravelled only to those who are fully competent for the highest Wisdom. That is the reason why Yājñavalkya would not discuss it in public. But he found in Ārtabhāga, who asked such a precise question, one competent enough to understand this secret and its inner Wisdom, and so he took him aside to teach in private. Ārtabhāga's competency at that moment was such that he needed only a *guru*'s guiding hand to pass on to the core of Wisdom, and so Yājñavalkya takes his hand and leads him to the finality of Wisdom. Such are the implications of the words, "Ārtabhāga, my dear, take my hand". It is not to be taken as the formal handshake of respect known to the West. It is the rare context of a *guru* helping his dear disciple pass the last lap of his journey toward Wisdom. Ārtabhāga finally found full satisfaction and he held his peace.

Karma understood here concerns not only human beings. Every being, whether living or not, is subject to it. The flowing of water, the burning of fire, the blowing of wind and all such events in Nature are part of it. These *karmas* are ordered together thus in order to cause the creation, sustenance and destruction of all living beings. Such phenomena, following laws of movement, are merely the expression of the creative urge of the total Nature. Electrons revolve round a nucleus and countless luminaries in the sky do likewise according to their own strict laws. This is how the world endures despite the unceasing changes taking place throughout it.

The meaning of *karma*, as normally understood, varies according to the context concerned. The rituals performed according to Vedic injunctions in order to propitiate certain gods (*deva*s) are called *karma*s. Then there are *karma*s that are supposed to cling to souls and result in their transmigration. They are usually classified into three — the past (*sañcita*), present (*prārabdha*) and future (*āgāmī*). All activities of day-to-day life are also called *karma*s. But none of these *karma*s need be considered praiseworthy in the context of Yājñavalkya passing Wisdom to Ārtabhāga. In that context, the reference to *karma* is made just after mentioning that the water, i.e. *Brahman*, consumes the fire of death. It is only natural to think that the praiseworthy *karma* referred to here is of *Brahman*, and can never be of any individual or thing. Likewise, the life and death of the person discussed here are to be seen as phenomenal appearances that take place in *Brahman* because of Its own self-unfolding *karma*. Such a view would also be in conformity with the basic message of Upaniṣads in general.

Now the only point to be clarified in the dialogue between Yājñavalkya and Ārtabhāga concerns the reference to good and bad actions. The *Bṛhadāraṇyaka Upaniṣad* says, "Verily, one becomes good by good actions, and bad by bad actions". The idea of meritorious and sinful actions falls within the context of Vedic rituals as well as in the context of *karma*s that supposedly cling to souls. But the Upaniṣad portrays *karma*s from a non-dual, absolutist stand. What is considered good actions here are the actions done with the understanding that one's capability to think, to make free decisions, and to act accordingly is merely an integral part of the total unfoldment of the creative urge or Nature abiding in the ultimate Reality. The unique character of such actions to be done can be decided upon after discerning the specific way in which Nature manifests Itself within oneself. One's actions should be fully in tune with this inner-Nature; such actions alone would make one happy. Such actions are called *svadharma* in *Gītā*. Even the thought of sin and virtue does not arise for actions thus performed. These are the kind of actions considered absolutely virtuous and acceptable to Upaniṣads. On the other hand, when one takes up the agency of actions and does them for benefit-motives, such actions are qualified as bad and render life a living hell. It must be this awareness that made Ārtabhāga feel fully satisfied and peaceful.

Notwithstanding all these clarifications, there is an enigma hidden in what happened between Ārtabhāga and Yājñavalkya. Going outside to have a privy talk, beyond even the scope of the written text, indicates this. This enigma is not merely peculiar to this particular question. It is an enigma that hides at the very core of the Wisdom of the Absolute (*brahma-vidyā*). Understanding the pure creativity (*karma*) of *Brahman* as the only remnant of a person, all of whose individuating factors merge with their corresponding cosmic ones, also entails the same enigma. This enigma is called *māyā* in Vedānta. That is the reason why Narayana Guru, when stating that the one Self, by assuming numerous forms, does all the *karma*s, adds that this is due to *māyā*.[8]

Now we know that all *karma*s take place in *Brahman* or in the total flow of Nature. When looked at from the point of view of the total Nature, there is neither virtuous action nor sinful action in It. There is only the incessant flow of action going on everywhere. But human beings normally evaluate these actions from their own point of view, which is already conditioned by various value concepts and social conventions. The classification

8 *Darśana-Mālā* VI.1.

of human actions as sinful and meritorious is the result of this kind of evaluation. What men take to be sinful actions or meritorious ones are really various expressed forms of the endless creative urge innate within the one Reality. The one through whom what we call sin is manifest is labelled a sinful person; and conversely, the one through whom what we consider virtue is manifest is labelled as a virtuous person. This is made unequivocally clear in *Bṛhadāraṇyaka* passage that we will examine next. Before entering it, it will be helpful to fix the place of the individual's *karma*s in the overall picture of the Upaniṣads' final teaching.

Karma and Brahman

Brahman, the ultimate Reality, is Existence (*sat*), Consciousness (*cit*) and Value Experience (*ānanda*) together as one. As Existence, it is the Substance behind all visible forms. As Consciousness, this Substance is alive and dynamic in essence, and is aware of all that happens within It. As Value Experience, even the most negligible of events in Consciousness are evaluated in terms of one's own happiness. The liveliness and dynamism of the Substance, when self-manifest, are called *karma*. Man should see his oneness with this Substance, which is always creative. The very same creativeness becomes manifest in the form of his activities too. Such is the ultimate meaning of one's *karma*s and even of one's life. This awareness establishes one fully in one's Self or *Brahman*. It also fully liberates one from all sense of sin and virtue; in Vedānta that state is called *mukti* (final Liberation). Such is the final teaching of all Upaniṣads as well as of *Bhagavad-Gītā*.

As this is the final teaching about the ultimate Reality, whatever is contrary to this belongs to the limbo of the unreal. The knowledge that leads us to the awareness of the one Reality is called *vidyā* (science), and that knowledge which leads us to mistake the unreal for the real is called *avidyā* (nescience). We come to the one and only ultimate Reality by *vidyā*; but endless are the false kinds of knowledge we arrive at by *avidyā*. The multiplicity of individuals and their souls, their birth, life and death, as well as their *karmas*, all these seem to be real only in the realm of *avidyā*. Hence the statements that appear in Upaniṣads and *Bhagavad-Gītā* regarding the birth and death of individuals, and the state after death, are meant to be understood as pertaining to the realm of *avidyā* and the unreal, and not as part of the final teaching. The scriptures are not meant for teaching the unreal. What they always insist on is the necessity of being aware of the one Reality. This Reality is never born nor does it ever die. Hence the one who knows the Real would not ask the question, "What will happen after death?"

As part of the enquiry into the one Reality, the unreal must unavoidably be considered so that it can be discriminated from the Real. This does not mean that such references are to be taken as part of the final teaching. To do so would in effect be violating the overall spirit of the scriptures. So, as a whole, scriptural passages concerning birth, death and the life after death are not to be treated as part of the teaching proper, but only as statements concerning the unreal. Indeed, what is unreal is to be negated finally, as when *Bṛhadāraṇyaka Upaniṣad* says, *neti neti* (not this, not this). Such discrimination is to be kept in mind when treating the scriptures. Otherwise, it would be as though we are entering a thick forest of words with no way out, as Śaṅkara puts it in his *Vivekacūḍāmaṇi* (The Crest Jewel of Discrimination).[9]

---

[9] See v. 62.

4

What Is Birth and Death?

Death, a Part of the Life Cycle

THE actual reference to death and life after death in *Bṛhadāraṇyaka Upaniṣad* appears in chapter IV, section 4 as part of a dialogue between Yājñavalkya and King Janaka. Passages 3 and 4 of this section read as follows:

> Just as a caterpillar, when it has come to the end of a blade of grass, draws itself together to another blade by taking the next step, so does this Self, after destroying this body, making it go into the unknown, draw itself together by taking another step.
>
> And as a goldsmith, taking a piece of gold, turns it into another newer and more beautiful shape, even so does this Self, after having destroyed this body and making it go into the unknown, make itself into another, newer and more beautiful shape like that of *pitṛs*, or of *gandharvas*, or of gods, or of Prajāpati, or of Brahmā or of other beings.[1]

The former stanza is very often quoted as a veritable scriptural evidence for the theory of reincarnation. At first glance it might appear to refer to the soul's passage from one body to another. But we see that this is not the case when examining it closely. Here the continuity of life portrayed is not intended to be envisioned with the first analogy alone. Both of the analogies have to be viewed together in order to understand the real

---

1 *Bṛhadāraṇyaka Upaniṣad* IV.iv.3-4.

intention of the Upaniṣadic *ṛṣi*. Often in the scriptures, one analogy is employed in order to compensate for what lacks in another given analogy.

We are all familiar with one or another kind of caterpillar that can walk across blades of grass. It bends its body upwards at the end of a blade of grass, pushes its head forward, fixes it on a new blade, and then pulls the tail end forward and thus finds itself on a new blade. When this example is taken separately it might seem that the caterpillar stands for the soul and the blades for bodies. But what is emphasized here is not the transmigration of souls, but the onward movement of the one and same Self-Reality; It leaves behind all older forms to acquire new ones. This is made more explicit in the next example.

The second analogy concerns a goldsmith who takes a piece of gold and gives it a newer, more beautiful shape. The former golden shape that disappears and the new one that appears stand for the changeful, visible forms or bodies assumed by Reality. Gold stands for Reality, which was never born and will never die. This Reality is not a soul hiding somewhere in the body; it is the all-pervading content in all bodies. The visible form of a gold piece may be altered any number of times without affecting its inner content. Likewise, one and the same Self-Reality ever endures while its older forms assumed become transformed into newer ones. This change of form happens because of the inner creative urge for becoming inherent in Reality; that urge is called *karma* in *Gītā*, as discussed previously.

What happens to the older forms? They disappear into the world of the unknown as is clearly stated in the text of the Upaniṣad. That means, they are no more to be known. When looked at from the point of view of an individual, the disappearance of an old form is called death, and the appearance of a new form is called birth. These events do not endanger the unity of Reality. Explained with the help of our analogy, the disappearance of an older golden ornament, and the appearance of a newer one, is not in fact two events. The event is the same. When looked at from the side of the older ornament-form it appears as death; while from the side of the newer form the same event is seen as birth. The death of a form in itself is the birth of another. That is how the life process endures without end. We are simply unaware of all its events or facets. The continuity of this life process is depicted by the analogy of a caterpillar; while the oneness of the enduring Reality existing in and through all changes of form is emphasized in the analogy of the gold worked by a goldsmith.

It becomes evident, when these two examples are put together and contemplated upon, that what is understood as *ātman* here is not an animating principle or spirit supposedly seated in the body. In this context, the etymological sense of the word becomes all the more meaningful. The word *ātman* is derived from the root *āp*, which means to pervade (*āp vyāpane*). *Ātman* thus means the invisible Reality or Substance that pervades all individuated visible forms, just as gold is the substance that pervades the visible form of all ornaments. This visible form, in the case of living beings, includes in it the physical phenomenon called the body as well as the phenomenon known as the soul.

Reality as abiding in the specific aspects is usually known as *ātmā* in Vedānta, and Reality as abiding in the universal or transcendent aspect as *Brahman* (the Absolute). The golden ornament can help us to visualize the sameness among all aspects; when it is known that gold is the existent substance of one ornament, it becomes evident that the same gold must be the substance in all ornaments. Likewise, upon realizing the Substance abiding as one's own individual existence, it becomes evident that the same abiding *Ātman* or Self exists as the Substance in all individual beings. Thus we come to see that both the individual or specific aspects and the universal or generic aspect of Reality have one and the same substanceless Substance abiding in them. The unity or non-duality of *Ātman* and *Brahman*, the most basic teaching of Vedānta, is to be understood in this sense. That is why the very next stanza of *Bṛhadāraṇyaka Upaniṣad* begins with one of the great dicta of Vedānta, stressing the oneness of *Ātman* and *Brahman*, namely, *sa vā ayam ātmā brahma* (this Self, being such, is *Brahman* indeed).

The meaning of death and the state after death, in the above-quoted stanza, should be understood within this wisdom context. The same gold continues to exist in and through various forms given it by the goldsmith. Seen from the side of the gold, it continually exists, giving it the possibility to appear in various forms, one after another. Seen from the side of the ornaments, old ones die as new ones are born each time the goldsmith plies his trade upon a form.

Were there a knowledge by which an ornament realizes, "I am gold", it would be called *vidyā* (science or right knowledge) in Vedānta. That knowledge by which the ornament would take itself as, "I am an ornament", is called *avidyā* (nescience or ignorance). Wise or ignorant, the same *Ātman*–Substance continues existing in and through all the world's changeful forms and in the animating principles of bodies called souls. When looked at from the point of view of the subsisting Reality, *Ātman* alone exists beginninglessly and endlessly. When looked at from the obverse side of the individual being, *ātman* is born and will die, and will be reborn again. The former kind of knowledge is called *vidyā* and the latter *avidyā*. The individual beings referred to here should be understood to include non-living entities as well.

The possibilities of the visible forms one *Ātmā* can assume are endless. Usually we categorize such beings in this world into the mineral kingdom, vegetable kingdom, animal kingdom, etc.

The human species is considered the highest rung of the animal kingdom. But are there beings higher than the human species? We may think there are no such beings since we can know nothing of them. But the limitation of our knowledge should never be considered the criterion for final judgement. The nature of the vegetable kingdom, as well as that of the animal kingdom, is unknown to those of the mineral kingdom. Similarly, other animals cannot understand the nature of being human. Even so, the human would never understand the nature and glory of beings above the human world, if there be any. So the incapacity of the human cannot be an honest criterion to assert or deny the existence of any being higher than the human species. That is the reason why the ancient *ṛṣi*s, rich in poetic imagination, conceived of beings such as *deva*s (gods), *pitṛ*s (manes) and *gandharva*s (divine musicians), and their concerned worlds. These beings and their worlds could be treated as merely imaginative musings or even as mental projections. Really, deciding which mental projections are fictitious and which ones are real would be an arduous, uncertain task. But let us remember that for the *ṛṣi*s, everything we see and even what we perceive to be materially real, is but mental projection of one Consciousness. Hence, instead of denying the existence of anything, the Upaniṣad admits the existence of everything as the manifest forms of one and the same Self. Such beings could be men, *pitṛ*s, *gandharva*s, *deva*s, *prajāpati*s (the Lords of beings), Brahmā the Creator, or any other being, living or not. That is to say, the same Self or *Ātman* subsists in all beings, from a mere grain of sand to the Creator of the World. This is emphatically stated in the next stanza after the one quoted above. It reads as follows:

> This Self, being such, is *Brahman* indeed. It becomes identified with understanding, mind, vital breath, sight, hearing, earth, water, air, space, light and absence of light, desire and absence of desire, anger and absence of anger, righteousness and absence of righteousness, and everything. Moreover, whatever is recognized

> here as "this", this Self subsists in it as the essence of "this" or the essence of "that". According as one functions, and according as one behaves, so does He (the Self) become. When one does good he becomes the doer of good. When one does evil he becomes the doer of evil. He becomes virtuous with virtuous actions, and he becomes bad with bad actions. Yet some say that a person is of the essence of desires. As is his desire so is his will. As is his will so is the deed he does. Whatever deed he does, that he attains.[2]

This passage needs no elucidation when viewed in the light of what was previously stated. It is the same Reality of the Self that abides in everything appearing in the world, whether good or bad, virtuous or non-virtuous. The same Self is equated to *Brahman* at the very beginning of the stanza. What appears in the form of understanding (*vijñāna*), mind (*manas*), life principle or vital breath (*prāṇa*), sight (*cakṣus*) and hearing (*śrotra*) in individual beings is nothing but the same Reality. Such gross universal factors as earth, water, air, space, etc. are also various manifest forms of the same Reality. Light (*tejas*) is a factor that could be understood to form both part of the individual and the gross universal aspects. As part of the individual, it is considered a person's lustre. As the gross and universal factor, it is fire. Even one who is labelled as a vicious person or evil-doer is an apparent form of the same Reality.

These are the ways that *karma*, or the creative urge inherent in the one Reality, manifests. It is with such a broad perspective that we have to understand the private conversation between Yājñavalkya and Ārtabhāga quoted earlier. To repeat the passage, "What they said was *karma*, what they praised was *karma*. Verily one becomes good by good actions, bad by bad actions."

The conversation between Yājñavalkya and Ārtabhāga quoted earlier, and the one between Yājñavalkya and Janaka quoted above, reveal the same basic principle. In the former

---

2 *Bṛhadāraṇyaka Upaniṣad* IV.iv.5.

case it was seen as the creative urge inherent in the ultimate Reality, and in the latter the emphasis was on the existentiality of the same. Reality is the same, but it is observed and referred to with reference to two different frames of reference.

The difference between them is only with respect to the points of view taken, and not of Reality viewed as such. Observing something and stating anything about it, by necessity, has to be done from some particular point of view, and the vision as well as the statement must have the colouration of that point of view. That is only one of the limitations of thought or language, but in no way does it affect the unity of Reality.

5

The Two Paths

THAT the departed souls go to higher regions, following either the path of *deva-yāna* (the path of gods) or of *pitr̥-yāna* (the path of manes), has become a well-established tenet in Indian religious thought. The soul that goes by the former path reaches the world of *Brahman* and does not come back to earth. The soul that goes by the latter path reaches the world of manes, wherefrom it again returns to earth by entering a woman's womb out of which it will be reborn. Such is the belief. Almost all the Purāṇas and Itihāsas (epics) take this idea for granted and therefore offer no critical examination of this idea of the two paths. Here we shall examine the original, most basic scriptures expressing this idea, that we might discover for ourselves the original intention of the *r̥ṣis* who conceived it.

An explicit reference to these two paths appears in *Chāndogya Upaniṣad* (V.10). The same two paths, with a slight change in details, are described in *Bhagavad-Gītā*, chapter VIII, where they are called the white path (*śukla-gati*) and the black path (*kr̥ṣṇa-gati*). We have first to examine the context in which this statement appears in *Chāndogya Upaniṣad* in order to see for ourselves what was really intended by the two paths mentioned in the Upaniṣad. The statements in any scripture are not meant to be understood after alienating them from the context in which they appear. The particular narration begins with section 3 of chapter V. It reads as follows:

Śvetaketu, the grandson of Aruṇa, went to an assembly of the Pāñcālas. Then Pravāhaṇa Jaivāli said to him, "Young man, has your father instructed you?" "Yes indeed, Venerable Sir" (said he in answer).

"Do you know to what place men go from here?" "No, Venerable Sir." "Do you know how they return again?" "No, Venerable Sir." "Do you know where the paths leading to the gods and leading to the manes separate?" "No, Venerable Sir."

"Do you know how that (yonder) world never becomes full?" "No, Venerable Sir." "Do you know how in the fifth libation water comes to be called a person?" "Indeed, Venerable Sir, no."

"Then why did you say that you had been instructed? Indeed how could anyone who did not know these things speak of himself as having been instructed?" Distressed, he went to his father's place and said to him, "Venerable Sir, you said indeed that you had instructed me without instructing me."

"That fellow of the princely class asked me five questions and I could not understand even one of them." He (the father) said, "As you stated to me these (questions) I do not know even one of them. If I had known them, how should I not have told them to you?"

Then Gautama went over to the king's place. To him, when he arrived, he (the king) had proper respect shown. In the morning he went up to the audience hall (where) the king said to him, "Venerable Gautama, choose a boon out of the wealth that belongs to the world of men." Then he replied, "Thine be the wealth of the world of men. O king, tell me that speech which you spoke to the young man." The king was perplexed.

"Stay for some time" he commanded him. Then he said to him, "As to what you have told me, Gautama, this knowledge has never reached the brāhmaṇas before you, therefore in all the worlds the rule (this teaching) belonged to the kṣatriya class only." Then he said to him:[1]

1 *Chāndogya Upaniṣad* V.iii.1-7.

This much constitutes section 3 of chapter V of the Upaniṣad. In the next section the king gives his answer to the five questions in the form of a new set of five fire-sacrifices (*pañcāgni-vidyā*).

Pañcāgni-vidyā, literally "the teaching on the five fires", forms part of the Vedic rituals. These fires are known as *dakṣiṇāgni, gārhapatyāgni, āhavanīyāgni, sabhyāgni* and *āvasathyāgni.* These five sacrificial fires are supposed to be maintained constantly by those who follow Vedism strictly. But this Vedic concept of the five sacrificial fires is subjected to a total revision here in the light of the wisdom of Vedānta. The result is the emergence of a new set of five fire sacrifices. The unknown realms of life and the known ones are correlated by means of these sacrifices. What emerges from the unknown realms, through different stages, causes the emergence of the individual human being. Its re-mergence back into the unknown Source is described likewise. So the emergence and re-mergence of individual beings are to be seen as part of this process. All these are symbolically represented as the new set of five fires taught by the King Pravāhaṇa. Let us see the nature of these sacrifices instructed to Gautama by the king.

Section 4

1. That world, verily, O Gautama, is a sacrificial fire, the sun itself the fuel, the rays the smoke, the day the flame, the moon the coals, the stars the sparks.
2. In this fire the gods offer (the oblation of) faith. From this offering arises Soma (the moon) the king.

Section 5

1. The god of rain, O Gautama, verily is the sacrificial fire; the air itself is its fuel, the cloud is the smoke, the lightning is the flame, the thunder the coals, and the thunderings the sparks.
2. In this fire the gods offer the libation of Soma the king. From this offering arises rain.

Section 6

1. The earth, verily, O Gautama, is the sacrificial fire; of this the year is the fuel, space is the smoke, the night is the flame, the quarters the coals, the intermediate quarters the sparks.
2. In this fire the gods offer the libation of rain. From this offering arises food.

Section 7

1. Man, verily, O Gautama, is the sacrificial fire; of this speech is the fuel, breath the smoke, the tongue the flame, the eyes the coals and the ears the sparks.
2. In this fire the gods offer the libation of food. From this offering arises semen.

Section 8

1. Woman, verily, O Gautama, is the sacrificial fire; of this the sexual organ is the fuel, what invites is the smoke, the vulva is the flame, what is done inside are the coals, the pleasure the sparks.
2. In this fire the gods offer the libation of semen. From this offering arises the foetus.

Section 9

1. For this reason indeed, in the fifth oblation water comes to be called man. This foetus enclosed in the membrane, having lain inside for ten or nine months or more or less, then comes to be born.
2. When born he lives whatever the length of his life may be. When he has departed, they (his friends) carry him to the appointed place for the fire (of the funeral pile), from which indeed he came, from which he arose.[2]

This last section apparently depicts the transference of a dead body to the funeral pyre. But this fire stands for the original

[2] *Chāndogya Upaniṣad* V.iv-ix.

sacrificial fire from which he arose, the primeval Source of the gradual creative process. That fire is the unknown world mentioned in section 4 above, which is none other than *Brahman*. It is to the fire that he is carried back. The sections that follow are to be understood in this light. The next section reads:

Section 10

1. So those who know this, and those who meditate in the forest on faith as austerity (or with faith and austerity) go to light and from light to day, from day to the bright half of the month (of the waxing moon), from the bright half of the month to those six months during which sun moves northward.
2. From these months to the year, from the year to the sun, from the sun to the moon, from the moon to the lightning. There, there is a person who is non-human. He leads them on to *Brahman*. This is the path leading to the gods.[3]

This path of the gods (*deva-yāna*) is followed, as clearly stated here, only by those who know the five-tiered sacrifice described earlier, as emphasized in the words "those who know this" (*tad ya ittham viduḥ*). This shows that an understanding of the five-tiered creation process, ending in the birth of an individual, gives one the capability to pursue the same path of knowledge to find one's own original Source. We notice that it is the gods who offer oblations at all five stages of the sacrifice. A god (*deva*) literally means a "bright entity" or "shining one"; and brightness or a bright entity stands for knowledge.

The above passages in the Upaniṣad indicate thus that it is one and the same knowledge everywhere that functions in the unfoldment of the many distinct individual beings out of the indistinct Reality, the Absolute or *Brahman* represented as the unknown other world in the Upaniṣad (see section 4 quoted

---

[3] *Chāndogya Upaniṣad* V.x.1-2.

above). The individual who emerges as a result of this unfoldment finds his or her identity with the original source by following backward the same path of knowledge (the path of *devas* or gods). Such is the implication of *deva-yāna* understood here. One and the same knowledge functions creatively in the emergence of the individual as well as in his understanding of this very process. The process of going back to the original Source through wisdom is figuratively represented as *deva-yāna*, the going back, which completes the cyclic function of knowledge or *devas*. This path of the gods is almost the same as *prati-prasava* (giving birth backwards) understood in the Yoga system. The entire scene is visualized here as a fire sacrifice (*yajña*). The onward process of giving birth as well as the backward process of re-merger takes place in the same Consciousness or *Brahman*. Thus the unknown Reality called *Brahman*, and the known entity of the person, are to be understood here as belonging to a holistic structural scheme of functional Consciousness. Such an understanding is the essence of Wisdom. The birth, life and death of individuals have their own role in this scheme. *Bhagavad-Gītā* also conceives of this cyclic scheme as *yajña* when it says:

> Food is the cause of beings and from rain food is produced; rain is produced from sacrifice, and sacrifice has its origin in action (*karma*).
>
> Know that *karma* arises from Brahmā (god of Creation) and that Brahmā traces his being to the Imperishable (*akṣara*). Therefore the all-pervasive Absolute (*Brahman*) is eternally well founded on sacrifice.
>
> He who fails to lead a life of hereunder, who does not conform to the rotation of such a wheel, such a man of vicious lifetime lives, O Pārtha, in vain indeed.[4]

What is understood as Wisdom (*jñāna*) in Vedānta is nothing

---

[4] *Bhagavad-Gītā* III.14-16.

short of a dawning awareness that one's own existence, along with existence *in toto,* belongs to the same cyclic process of becoming, which itself occurs in the same Consciousness or Reality. This way of Wisdom is figuratively called here *deva-yāna* as the word *deva* stands for Wisdom or brightness and *yāna* for path. *Pañcāgni-vidyā* mentioned here in this Vedāntic context is not intended to be understood as the five rituals of Vedism, as already noticed. Here the Vedic five-ritual concept becomes subjected to a total revision and revaluation in the light of Vedāntic Wisdom. The gods, within this Vedāntic context, stand for the causal Consciousness that becomes subject to a fivefold becoming, figuratively conceived of as five sacrifices. The emergence of a person is the final result of this fivefold becoming. Such a person will rely on that same causal Consciousness (gods) to trace himself back to his primeval source. Such is *deva-yāna* of *Chāndogya Upaniṣad.*

Everything in this world emerges from and merges back into *Brahman;* this is a fundamental tenet of Vedānta. The five burnt sacrifices and the return to *Brahman* via *deva-yāna* are simply poetic imageries symbolizing the individual's emergence from and re-mergence into *Brahman* or the ultimate Reality. Let it be noted that the process of going back to *Brahman* is also five-tiered like the *pañcāgni-vidyā* conceived of. It covers light, time (from day to year), sun, moon and lightning. According to this Upaniṣad it is the individual, not his/her soul alone, that emerges from and merges back into *Brahman.* This is the truth of everyone's life, enlightened or not, but is understood so by *jñānī*s alone. It appears irrelevant to most merely because they are unaware of this secret concerning *Brahman* and Its creativity as well as themselves.

Not everyone is capable to attain this Wisdom. Instead of understanding the five rituals metaphorically, they perform these rituals in strict accordance with the Vedic injunctions. Then they await the fruits of these actions, in this world and the hereafter. They are called the *ajñānīs*. They do not care to know the cyclic nature of life or its underlying Reality.

Such people have their own ideas about life, in the now and the hereafter. The life-concept of *ajñānīs* is also metaphorically and summarily depicted in the following stanzas of the Upaniṣad. It is given the name *pitṛ-yāna*. It is stated at the very beginning of the stanza that this is the view of the ignorant; living in villages, they perform all Vedic rituals and do works of public utility. The passage reads:

> But those, who in the village practise sacrifices and perform works of public utility and alms-giving, they pass into the smoke, from smoke to night, from night to the dark fortnight of the month, from the dark fortnight of the month to the six months in which the sun moves southward, but they do not reach the year.
>
> From those months to the world of the manes (*pitṛs*), from the world of the manes to space, from space to the moon. That is the King Soma. That is the food of the gods that the gods eat.
>
> Having dwelt there till the time of falling down, they return again by that course by which they came to space, from space into air; and after having become the air they become the smoke; after having become smoke they become mist.
>
> After having become mist they become cloud; after having become cloud it rains down. They are born here as rice and barley, herbs and trees, as sesamum plants and beans. Thence the release becomes extremely difficult, for whoever eats the food and emits semen he becomes like unto him.
>
> Those whose conduct here has been good will quickly attain a good birth, the birth of a brāhmaṇa, the birth of a kṣatriya or the birth of a vaiśya. But those whose conduct here has been evil, will quickly attain an evil birth, the birth of a dog, the birth of a hog, or the birth of a *cāṇḍāla*.[5]

---

[5] *Chāndogya Upaniṣad* V.x.3-7.

This is *pitṛ-yāna* (the path of manes) described in *Chāndogya Upaniṣad*. All its details are diametrically opposed to those of *deva-yāna*. *Deva-yāna* is really the correct way of understanding life and death. This is the path of a *jñānī*. Conversely, *pitṛ-yāna* is the path taken to be true by an *ajñānī*. The understanding an *ajñānī* has about himself will always be wrong. In other words, he is not aware of life's real nature because he mistakes his wrong notions, self-created or imparted by other ignorant ones, to be the real nature of life. This is the fate of those who run after Vedic rituals (*karma-mārga*). Of course, even when the ignorant has wrong ideas about life, its real nature remains unchanged. That means, an ignorant man's idea about life is not true even in his own case. It is merely a wrong notion in his mind. It is thus to be presumed that the path named *pitṛ-yāna* is not even true in the case of those who believe it is. It only means that certain individuals have such a wrong notion in their mind and live accordingly. So *pitṛ-yāna* of this Upaniṣad is taken to be true by those who believe in it.

Commentators and translators of this Upaniṣadic passage often interpolate the words "as long as there is the residue of good actions" betwixt the words "having dwelt there" and "till the time of falling down" (from the world of the moon). Such an interpolation is unwarranted here. The original words *yāvat sampātam uṣitvā* only mean, "having dwelt there till the time of falling down". Such extraneous and incorrect interpolations make the wrong notion of the ignorant all the more complex.

A Third Path

Chāndogya Upaniṣad describes a third path in addition to *deva-yāna* and *pitṛ-yāna*. It is merely called the third position (*tṛtīyam-sthānam*). The stanza following the previous one quoted reads:

> But on neither of these ways are those small creatures which are continually revolving through birth and death. Their's is the third state. By this it comes about that the world becomes not full.

Therefore let one detest it.[6]

What is stated here is neither the case of a *jñānī* nor of an *ajñānī*. A *jñānī* understands the real as the real. An *ajñānī* understands the unreal as the real. Human beings come under either one of these two categories. But there are beings that do not have any understanding of life at all. They are small creatures. They are born, they live and they die. They are not worried about the meaning of birth and death and the state after death. The cyclic process of life continues through them. This process has no beginning or end. They do not reach any other world. That is why that world does not become overfull. Human beings are recommended to detest this state. The life of small creatures is not guided by any understanding of the meaning of life. Such a life is not life for human beings to follow. For that reason only, the life of small creatures is detestable to man.

Even this third state is often interpreted as the state attained by those humans who follow neither of the two paths described previously. But the Upaniṣad evidently intends only to describe the state of other "small creatures" that do not habitually think of the meaning of life.

The Paths of Jñānīs and Ajñānīs

Do *jñānī*s take one path after death and *ajñānī*s another? If that were so, we would have to say that the ultimate Reality taught in the Upaniṣads is not applicable to all irrespectively. But the Upaniṣads teach that there is only one ultimate Reality. Every being, living or not, has its emergence, existence and re-mergence in the same Reality. It is from the same Reality that both *jñānī* and *ajñānī* emerge, and into it both re-merge. To say that this final teaching holds true only for a *jñānī* is sheer nonsense. The reality of life is true in respect to *jñānī* and *ajñānī* alike. Now the life after death, for a *jñānī* or *ajñānī*, according to

6 *Chāndogya Upaniṣad* V.x.8.

the Upaniṣadic teachings, must be examined and understood in the light of this general teaching on the overall nature of life. *Taittirīya Upaniṣad* poses this problem directly. This question is asked in the form of an auxiliary question after the main theme of the Upaniṣad has been presented. The disciple asks:

> Does anyone who knows not, when departing from this life, go to the yonder world? Or is it that one, someone who knows, on departing from this life, attains that world?[7]

The question asked here is but one in number, but it is presented in the Upaniṣad as a plural by using the word *anupraśnāḥ* (auxiliary questions), as if many questions are involved in this one question. It is true that a volley of questions arises from this one question. The present writer in his commentary on *Taittirīya Upaniṣad* gives a detailed examination of the answer given to this question. Here we will present but the gist of the Upaniṣad's answer.

There is no need for any differentiation between the wise and the ignorant in this respect. Both were non-existent in the beginning. Both came out of the one and same Reality as a result of Its own proper activity (*sukṛtam*). That Reality is neither expressible by word nor graspable by mind. One who knows that Reality is not worried by such thoughts as "Why didn't I do good deeds?" or "Why did I do evil deeds?" For him, those who are called the wise as well as the ignorant, and what is known as death as well as life after death, and what is called here and the hereafter are all unreal. This is the tone of the answer given in the Upaniṣad.

In other words, those who ask such questions are not fully aware of the Reality expounded in the Upaniṣad. They are prompted to ask such questions by virtue of their ignorance. Therefore, the ignorance in the mind of the questioner that prompts such a question must first be removed. The ultimate

---

7 *Taittirīya Upaniṣad* II.vi.1.

nature of life that any Upaniṣad teaches is true for all, irrespective of one's wisdom or ignorance. The only difference is that the wise know that Reality while the ignorant do not. Whether one knows it or not, Reality remains ever the same. Both the wise and ignorant live and die in one and same world, according to one and same inherent laws of becoming and destruction. One of the initial questions asked by Pravāhaṇa to Śvetaketu was, "Do you know where the paths leading to the gods and leading to the manes separate?" (see verse V.iii.2 quoted above). No direct answer to this question is given in the Upaniṣad. The presumable answer would be, "it is where *jñāna* and *ajñāna* separate".

A scholarly understanding of the Upaniṣads and their commentaries will not necessarily remove one's fundamental ignorance. Even the recondite ability to write commentaries on these scriptures does not remove this ignorance. I once experienced an interesting incident that demonstrated this. A research scholar who was engaged in studying the philosophy of a Malayalam version of *Rāmāyaṇa* by Ezhuthacchan once came to me for a final bit of advice to polish his soon-to-be-submitted doctoral thesis. The philosophy of life and death as presented in *Rāmāyaṇa* was fully and beautifully elucidated in the thesis and supported by relevant quotes and explanations from the Upaniṣads, *Bhagavad-Gītā* and other basic textbooks of Vedānta. The scholar's thesis demonstrated that he had indeed carefully scrutinized all these texts and presented a clear understanding of their philosophy. On finishing reading the thesis, the scholar asked me:

"Swamiji, I have a question to ask you."

"All right."

"What happens to a soul after death?"

"Didn't we answer this question in detail in your thesis?"

"Yes Swamiji, I know that answer. But this is for my

personal clarification."

This shows that the philosophy he was studying and writing about had not become his own nor yet solved his personal problems.

Some people will continue asking the same question even after having the truth explained to them a number of times. There is only one way to silence them, and that is to tell them a story befitting the world of ignorance they live in.

In fact, the stories of *pitṛ-yāna* and *deva-yāna*, along with the assumption of two worlds in which the wise and the ignorant each supposedly go upon death, were created by some ṛṣis, especially of the Purāṇas and Itihāsas, in order to satisfy those still in the world of ignorance. Such tales are not to be taken as forming part of the final teaching of the scriptures.

6

In Kaṭha Upaniṣad

Kaṭha Upaniṣad teaches *brahma-vidyā*, with the problem of life after death as the central theme. Stanza 4 of section 5 of this Upaniṣad says:

> When the embodied one, that dwells within' drops the body down and becomes released from it, what does then remain? This, verily is that.[1]

That which remains or continues to exist is the absolute Reality (*Brahman*). Every being has for its self-content this very same Reality. The nature of this Reality was elucidated in a previous stanza as follows:

> The all-knowing One (the Self) is never born nor does It die. It is not originated from anywhere, nothing originates from It either. Unborn, everlasting, eternal, the most ancient, It is not destroyed on the destruction of the body.[2]

The ultimate Reality, subsisting in all the entities of the world, is not destroyed by the destruction of the visible form that we call the body. If we identify ourselves with the Reality within us, we, as that Reality, have no birth and death, because that Reality was never born and never will die. This is the basic stand of the Upaniṣad. The question of life after death has also to be seen from the same basic standpoint. If we use the analogy of *Chāndogya*

---

1. *Kaṭha Upaniṣad* V.4.
2. Ibid. II.18.

Upaniṣad, when a goldsmith gives a new form to an old ornament, the old ornament is dead. But the gold in it continues to exist in the form of the new ornament. Where could the old ornament go at its death other than into the gold? The old ornament had gold, not its form, for its subsisting reality. Even so, man exists neither with vitality, nor soul, nor the physical body as the subsisting reality. These are merely facets of his visible form. What subsists in him, as with the gold in the ornament, is the Reality that has in it the potential to appear as the soul as well as the body at once. This is also explicitly stated in the Upaniṣad thus:

> Not by any *prāṇa* or *apāna* does any mortal whatever live. But by another do they live on which these (*prāṇa* and *apāna*) both depend.[3]

Neither *prāṇa* nor *apāna* nor the body is the subsisting Reality that exists and lives in and as all beings. These are all aspects of the visible form in which Reality manifests itself. These are not eternal. What will happen, then, when these visible aspects disappear at the event we call death? The Reality that was subsisting in and through these visible forms will continue to exist in new specific forms. That is how the world endures in spite of the disappearance of every entity in it.

All this is stated clearly in the Upaniṣad, after which Yama the *guru* then tells Naciketas what will happen to the self after death. But along with it, he teaches the mystery of the birthless and deathless Reality. Yama says:

> Look here, I shall explain to you the mystery of *Brahman*, the eternal, and also how the self fares after reaching death, O Gautama.[4]

Here Yama is going to show Naciketas two mutually exclusive positions. One concerns the birthless and deathless *Brahman*, and

---

3 *Kaṭha Upaniṣad* V.5.

4 Ibid. V.6.

the other, what happens to the soul after death. The question, "what happens after death?" is relevant only where death is real. Where death is real, the birthless and deathless *Brahman* is unreal. It is because man always lives in fear of death that man alone is called *martya* (the mortal) in Sanskrit, even though all beings are mortal. So in the present context of *Kaṭha Upaniṣad*, man is also called *martya*.

That death is the end of life, only because of *avidyā* (ignorance) will not be repeated here. Yama answers the question of how the soul fares after death, in a way that does not form part of the Wisdom teaching. Such an answer merely forms part of the realm of ignorance and is given to satisfy the ignorant who will go on asking this question. They are incapable of realizing the Wisdom of *Brahman*. Yet the mystery of *Brahman* is the real Wisdom teaching. Yama's statement on how the soul fares after death is actually confined to only one verse. The rest of the section is wholly devoted to the birthless and deathless Reality of *Brahman*. It is thus clear that the statement on life after death will be taken seriously by the ignorant, and that of Wisdom will be taken seriously by the true seeker. Both cannot be true for the same person! Unless we approach these verses with such discrimination we will surely be misled.

Yama tells how the self fares after death in the next verse, but this telling can only satisfy the ignorant. It reads:

> Some enter into a womb for embodiment; others enter stationary objects according to their deeds and according to their knowledge.[5]

Evidently, when considered along with the entire context of the Upaniṣad, this statement does not form part of the central teaching, but is only a picture of life after death that could be imagined by an ignorant one. The real teaching on the immortal Reality is given in the very next verse. It reads:

---

5 *Kaṭha Upaniṣad* V.7.

> That Person who is awake even in those who are asleep, who shapes himself as he desires, that indeed is the pure. That is *Brahman*, that indeed is called the immortal. All the worlds have This for their basis. No one ever transgresses It. This, verily, is that.[6]

We thus conclude that references to life after death appearing in the Upaniṣads are imageries suggested by our *ṛṣi*s to satisfy the clouded minds of the ignorant, or to gently guide them out of their ignorance, from the standpoint of their own preconditioning. That is the real reason why such pictures differ from scripture to scripture. That which is imaginary could take any shape. What is real can have no such variety. But these imaginary pictures suggested by the *ṛṣi*s somehow became fixed ideas in the minds of the ignorant.

Yet the fixed idea of reincarnation has a positive value of its own. Since death is something real in the eyes of the ignorant, the idea of reincarnation helps them maintain a belief in the immortality of the Self while at least giving the hope of attaining it some time in the unknown future. The idea that the nature of the next birth is decided by one's *karma*s done during this birth also compels its believers to live their lives by doing good *karma*s; thus it has a potent ethical value.

That the attainment of immortality occurs after death is yet another idea that became fixed in the minds of the ignorant, as a corollary to the idea of rebirth. Immortality (*amṛtatva*) means deathlessness. Is it not meaningless to say that deathlessness is attained "after" death? The deathless has no death and it has no "after" death. The immortality taught by *Kaṭha Upaniṣad*, as well as by other Upaniṣads, is the immortality where birth and death are meaningless, and is to be attained here in this world itself. Neither the idea of death nor of the state after death worries the one who has attained immortality here and now. Both are unreal for him.

---

6 *Kaṭha Upaniṣad* V.8.

Naciketas approached Yama with the problem concerning life after death. But as the Upaniṣad ends, it says:

> Naciketas, then, having gained this wisdom . . . as imparted by death, attained *Brahman*, and became free of the changefulness of becoming and free from death."

Having realized immortality, he became free of the problem also.

7

In Bhagavad-Gītā

Bhagavad-Gītā is a frequently quoted scripture used to support the theory of reincarnation. The idea is seemingly suggested within different contexts of *Gītā*. The most quoted passages are taken from chapter II. Yet it is important to note that these passages are always preceded by the emphasis that *Ātmā* is the one, all-underlying Reality that is both unborn and deathless. Verse 20 of chapter II says:

> That (Reality) is never born, nor does It die; once having been, It does not cease to be either. Unborn, eternal, perpetual, ancient, It is not destroyed at the destruction of the body.[1]

Hence, any reference that follows must obviously be taken as subservient to this primary or foundational stand. Immediately succeeding the above verse follows the most quoted verse used in support of reincarnation. It reads as:

> The born, for sure, will die;
> The dead, for sure, has to be born;
> Therefore over the inevitable
> You should not grieve.[2]

The connotation of this verse can only be revealed after determining how one perceives oneself and what one identifies oneself to be. If one identifies oneself with the birthless and deathless *Ātmā*, then the question of rebirth never arises.

---

1 *Bhagavad-Gītā* II.20.

2 Ibid. II.27.

If I identify with the apparent form (*bhāva*), the apparent form, even after being taught that I am the immortal *Ātmā*, then I am still to be counted among the ignorant persons to whom birth is real, death is real, and consequentially rebirth also. The above verse forms a section of verses (II.26-28) that relate to the unreal world of appearances. In this realm, the emergence of one apparent form always involves the disappearance of some previous apparent form. This alternating process of the birth and death of apparent forms goes on endlessly. For example, if a gold artisan heats an ornament and begins to reshape it, the disappearance of the old ornamental form obviously involves the appearance of a new one. Many forms will be assumed by the same gold over the years, as gold must always assume some form. Likewise, without assuming the ever-changing apparent form of the world, the absolute Substance *Ātman* does not exist either. If I take this world appearance as what is ultimately real, then naturally both birth and death will endlessly appear real. The above verse emphasizes that one still need not grieve even if *bhāva* of Reality is taken to be real, because in that realm birth and death are inevitable. Evidently this section does not form part of *Gītā*'s essential teaching that is revealed immediately beforehand in the same chapter. The essential teaching is given in this section from an existential (*sat*) point of view, where *Ātmā* alone is to be perceived as existing.

Another famously quoted verse used in support of the reincarnation theory reads as follows:

> As a man casting off his worn out garments receives new ones, likewise the soul casting aside the worn out bodies takes to others that are new.[3]

To many, this verse apparently teaches that a soul leaves one body when it is outworn and then receives a new one. If we interpret it in this sense, then this verse would mean that there

---

3 *Bhagavad-Gītā* II.22.

must be as many souls as there are bodies. But a more strict interpretation of this verse yields the verity that bodies are many and the embodied is one. The plural word *śarīrāṇī* (bodies) is used to denote the bodies and the singular word *dehī* is used in respect of the embodied. The plural or singular forms of each, and their significance, seem to have been missed by many commentators. Upon scrutinizing the structure of these words, it becomes obvious that this verse expresses the embodied as one while the bodies are many.

It need not be pointed out that the idea that there are multiple souls is itself caused by ignorance according to the philosophy of Advaita Vedānta. In fact, we get a completely different picture of this verse when we interpret it in the light of the philosophy of Vedānta, as well as when we interpret it according to the line of thought expressed in both the preceding and succeeding verses. The analogy of the golden ornament of *Chāndogya Upaniṣad* can greatly assist us here. In this analogy, the gold (of the golden ornament) represents *dehī* (embodied one), and the ornamental shape it assumes represents *deha* or *śarīra*. So gold assumes the shape of an ornament. Though this ornamental form or body does not endure forever, the gold in it does. This gold has to and will exist in some form or another seemingly forever. Any gold put before us, in the shape of an ornament, must have assumed countless forms before appearing in its present one. Likewise, we can conjecture it will assume countless forms in the future. So the same gold exists enduringly while its form changes endlessly. When one form is changed into another, this event could be treated as the death of a former form and the birth of a new one. Gold here is to be understood in the place of the eternal Self; and the ornaments formed in an endless succession are to be understood in place of the bodies the Self assumes. Therefore the gold gives up an old form just as a man casts off his old garments. It takes a new form just as the same man puts on new garments. Just as the same man continues to exist while his garments are changed, the same Reality continues to exist forever while its visible forms constantly change. Furthermore, the overall context in which this stanza appears does not relate to a consideration of life and death, but rather to the discrimination between the eternal and transient aspects of Existence, and their value. The imperishable nature of the Reality is actually described in the preceding verses. For example, verse 17 of the same chapter says:

> Know That to be indestructible by which all this is pervaded. None can bring about the destruction of This that knows no decrease.[4]

When we re-examine verse 22 in the light of all this, we will no longer see the portrait of reincarnation so commonly presented to us. Instead we see the portrait of Nature's eternal flow, in all its multiplicity and changefulness, of which all births and deaths form a part, taking place in one eternal and changeless Reality. We can then paraphrase the verse as follows:

> Just as a man casts off his outworn garments and receives new ones, so does the embodied (Reality) cast off outworn bodies, and assumes new ones. (Our words.)

That one Reality continues to exist despite all changes is indicated in the very next verse as:

> Weapons do not cut This, fire does not burn This, water does not wet This, and wind does not dry This.[5]

As stated earlier, the aim of this part of *Gītā* is to help Arjuna or the seeker to discriminate between the eternal and transient aspects of life, as well as to not worry over the birthless and deathless *sat,* nor life's unavoidable exigencies within its transient *bhāvas*. Any reference to life after death would be out of place in this overall context. Actually, any reference to life and death as commonly understood does not match this context.

---

4 *Bhagavad-Gītā* II.17.

5 Ibid. II.23.

We have discussed how some interpreters see in this verse the idea of reincarnation by interpolating certain preconceived ideas, accumulated elsewhere, into the text. What is important though is to decide whether this idea of reincarnation was the intention of the original author. Authors like Vyāsa will never say something irrelevant to the context under discussion in basic texts like *Gītā*. The relevancy and meaning of any scriptural statement is intended to be understood in the light of the given context in which it falls, as well as the overall message of that scripture. No verse is meant to be torn from its context and then construed by interpolating one's own preconceived ideas into the text. In effect, such interpretations often do injustice to the original author.

The Case of Yoga-Bhraṣṭa

Another portion of *Gītā*, where reincarnation is actually made mention of, is in chapter VI, verses 37-42. This chapter, called Dhyāna-Yoga, deals with unitive contemplation. The ideal human life according to *Gītā* is that of a *yogī* or a *yoga-yukta* (one who is united with *yoga*). Chapter VI shows how one's life can be progressively transformed into a unitive contemplation that culminates in complete *yoga*. As such, one becomes a real *yogī*. Verse 36 makes it perfectly clear that without a subdued mind one cannot attain this goal. At this point Arjuna asks a question:

> What path does he take whose mind, unsubdued, but endowed with faith, has deviated from *yoga*, not reaching to yogic attainments?[6]

Arjuna further clarifies this question in the next two verses. Kṛṣṇa then answers him in verses 40-42 by saying:

> O Arjuna, neither here nor hereafter is there destruction for him, for none of propitious efforts ever goes to perdition.

---

6 *Bhagavad-Gītā* VI.37.

> Having attained to the world of the meritorious and having dwelt there for countless years, he who deviated from the path of *yoga* is reborn in a house of the pure and well-to-do.
>
> Else he is born in a family of wise *yogī*s only. A birth like this is very rare to obtain in this world.[7]

Reincarnation is seemingly taken for granted by Kṛṣṇa here. But we have to notice, to whom does reincarnation happen? *Jñānī*s or *yoga-yukta*s, described at the conclusion of the same chapter, always live with their inner self merged in the ultimate Reality. They meditate on *Brahman* in full faith. As mere phenomena, birth and death are never feared in the case of such *yogī*s. They know themselves as one with the absolute Substance and Its functional nature. Arjuna's question regards those seekers who are not yet fully in line with the path of *yoga*. They are referred here to as *yoga-bhraṣṭa*s (those who deviate from *yoga*). They are not *jñānī*s. They do not have the experiential awareness of the one Reality that is beyond birth and death. Birth and death still seem to be real for them. They also worry about the hereafter. Since such problems form part of their ignorance, the answers to such problems must be framed in such a way that is understandable to their ignorant minds, so as not to confuse them all the more. Meanwhile, the door of wisdom is left open to them, and the hope for immortality is retained. Kṛṣṇa himself, in verse III.29, says that the wise should not disrupt the thinking of the ignorant, who remain attached to *karma*s.

Gītā statement regarding reincarnation is also thus not to be taken as the real nature of life, but instead to belong to the unreal nature of life. Kṛṣṇa answered a common question arising in the minds of the ignorant by making use of a deeply rooted belief pattern in those same minds. As such, he is able to give them a convincing and hopeful answer.

---

7 *Bhagavad-Gītā* VI.40-42.

As Part of the Perishable

The next seeming reference to reincarnation appears in the eighth chapter of *Gītā*, the Akṣara-Brahma-Yoga (the Imperishable Absolute Unitively Understood). This chapter discriminates between the perishable and imperishable aspects of the Absolute, and treats them unitively. This is done for the sake of helping the seeker both know the imperishable Reality and see his oneness with the manifest existence of that imperishable Reality. The two paths of *deva-yāna* and *pitr̥-yāna*, discussed in *Chāndogya Upaniṣad*, also find their place in *Gītā* under the names of *śukla-gati* and *kr̥ṣṇa-gati*, with some minor alterations. This has already been adequately discussed, as directly related to the passage in *Chāndogya Upaniṣad*, and need not be repeated here.

There is no need to reiterate that birth and death are real only in the world of perishable phenomena; thus these two paths a soul might take after death are not intended to pertain to the imperishable Reality. They are relevant only within the perishable aspect of Reality. There can be no such problem in the realm of the imperishable Reality, as there is no coming and going there. That is why, after detailing the two paths, Kr̥ṣṇa closes the chapter by saying:

> The *yogī* who understands the basic nature of these two paths is not confounded at all. Therefore at all times be a *yogī*, O Arjuna.[8]

Kr̥ṣṇa implies that these two paths here are pertinent only within the realm of the unreal and so Arjuna need not be confounded; rather, he is to always be a *yogī*. That means these two paths also do not form the essential teaching of *Gītā* or the true nature of life. They are only to be seen as forming part of the *kṣara* world. So *Gītā* teaches: do not be confounded by what happens in the perishable world; instead identify yourself with the imperishable Reality.

---

8 *Bhagavad-Gītā* VIII.27.

One Īśvara Alone Continues

Lastly, chapter XV seemingly refers again to the problem of reincarnation in verses 7-8. They read:

> In this world of living beings My own tiny but eternal
> portions, having become living beings, attract
> to them the senses, of which the mind is the sixth,
> which abide in Nature.
>
> When *Īśvara* assumes a body and when He abandons
> it, He takes these (mind and senses) and moves forward
> even as the wind gathers fragrances from its abodes.[9]

Upon scrutiny, we can see that this verse does not necessarily imply that souls leave old bodies to take up new ones, as it is often interpreted. To see why this is so, one should understand the first verse of this chapter, which portrays the tree of functional consciousness, with its roots on high and branches reaching downward. Each living being is said to be a leaf of this tree, where the tree stands for the eternality of life. The minute qualitative elements in the same ultimate Reality (*mama eva aṁśaḥ*) appear in the form of individual living beings (*jīva-bhūtaḥ*) due to the creative vitality (*prakṛti*) inherent in It. Each being's individuality is decided by his mind and senses, which again are derived from the same creative vitality called *prakṛti*. As discussed earlier, this *prakṛti* was equated to *karma* in chapter VIII, verse 3 of *Gītā*.

The Absolute or *Brahman*, when endowed with the creative urge, is called *Īśvara*, which literally means "the controller". This creative Reality ever discards its minute forms and assumes new ones, thereby ensuring a novelty to the eternal flux of life. Such is the picture of life represented in these two verses. Often the word *Īśvara* is taken to mean a soul, or is even mistranslated as "the soul bound to its *karmas*". That means the theory of

---

9 *Bhagavad-Gītā* XV.7-8.

reincarnation is often read into these verses without any concern for the literal sense, and without reference to the general nature of the chapter, let alone the overall message of *Gītā*. This in no way does justice to the original author.

The unfoldment of *Īśvara*'s incessant creative urge is called *karma*. *Īśvara*, as the one Reality, under the process of this unfoldment, is called *prakṛti*. As part of His creative advancement, He takes up the individuating adjuncts of living beings, like mind and senses. This process is compared to a wafting wind gathering the fragrance of flowers. The source of the fragrance here is none but *prakṛti*. Portrayed as such, an individual's life is to be seen as part of the total flow of creative becoming. This verse neither mentions nor suggests that a soul wafts mind and senses from one body to another. The same *Īśvara* always continues to exist. As part of *Īśvara*'s advancement, His minute elements or parts emerge in the forms of beings, and then re-merge after some time. Those elements also have in them the same inner urge for advancement as *Īśvara*. It could be the word *jīva* in the compound words *jīvaloke* and *jīvabhūta* in verse XV.7 quoted above that made the interpreters see a reference to a "soul" here. Really the word *jīva* means just "a being that sustains through breathing" (*jīva prāṇa-dhāraṇe*), and thus it is equivalent to the English term "living organism." *Jīva* therefore refers here to "an individual." The compound word *jīvaloke* means "in the world of living beings", and *jīvabhūta*, "having become individuals". So as an individual, I am a *jīva*; you are a *jīva*; to say I have a *jīva* within me is wrong.

In short, the theory of reincarnation does not form part of the essential teaching of *Gītā* or the Reality governing life that it depicts. The reincarnation theory is often read too deeply into *Gītā* and is even considered crucial due to the misinterpretation of certain verses, or by mistaking the unreal, as *Gītā* refers to it, for the real.

8

In Brahma-Sūtras

THERE are allusions to the idea of reincarnation in parts of *Brahma-Sūtras* of Bādarāyaṇa. Section 3 of chapter 3 describes how a soul, in accord with its *karmas*, will fare after death. The idea that *prārabdha-karma* (*karma* already initiated) must be completed even by liberated souls is mentioned in *sūtra* 15 of section 1, chapter 4. Chapter 4 also describes and differentiates *parā-vidyā* (transcendental knowledge) from *aparā-vidyā* (non-transcendental knowledge), and explains how either kind of knowledge will help one gain *para-Brahman* or *apara-Brahman*, respectively.

Section 1 of chapter 3 supposedly describes life after death. And section 3 of the same chapter shows how the soul who worships or meditates on *Brahman* attains liberation.

Sūtra III.1.1 is supposed to expound the transmigratory nature of souls. The original *sūtra* reads:

> *tad-antara-pratipattau ramhati samparisvaktaḥ praśnanirūpaṇābhyām*[1]

The usual translation of this *sūtra* runs:

> In obtaining a different (body) (the soul) goes enveloped (by subtle parts of the elements), (as appears from) question and explanation.

In his comments on this *sūtra*, Śaṅkara says,

> It depicts the theory that a soul leaves one body along with its chief vital energy (*mukhya-prāṇa*), senses, mind, *avidyā*, *karma* and

[1] *Brahma-Sūtras* III.i.1.

knowledge of the previous state of existence and attains a new one.

But we neither come across the word *jīva,* nor the word *śarīra,* in the text of the original *sūtra*. These words, along with the idea of a soul leaving one body with its *mukhya-prāṇa,* senses, etc. for another, are interposed. With such an interposing of words by Śaṅkara, the idea of soul-transmigration is presumed.

If we eliminate such interpolated words and ideas, and then try to make sense of the *sūtra,* we get a completely different picture. That picture would present an onward progression of life as a whole. Compare the original without interpolation:

> In obtaining a different, goes enveloped; by question and explanation.

Or it could be read:

> On obtaining difference, goes enveloped, from question and explanation.

As such, the original *sūtra* could be more accurately paraphrased or understood as follows:

> When the one existent Reality, as part of life's onward flow, leaves behind one state to assume another, It pushes forward as a whole. We understand this from questions posed in the Upaniṣads and the answers that follow. (Our words.)

The *sūtra* in question, as generally agreed upon by most commentators, tries to bring into relief the implication of stanza 4.iv.3 of *Bṛhadāraṇyaka Upaniṣad,* which we have already examined.[2] In this passage, the onward flow of life is compared to the movement of a caterpillar from one blade of grass to another. We previously noted just how far commentators misconstrued this Upaniṣadic passage. Without the aid of interposed words or ideas, we can see how this Upaniṣadic passage is in agreement with the non-interposed *Brahma-Sūtras* passage above.

[2] See pages 31-32 above.

The primeval Reality is that which ever exists. That is why It is called *sat* in Vedānta, which literally means "existence." Vedānta says that Reality is pure Consciousness in essence, and so *sat* is also *cit*. *Cit* means "Consciousness". That which is Consciousness in essence, or Consciousness as Reality, never remains inert. It is always alive and creative. This creativity results in the constant emergence of new forms while older ones vanish. The concept of *karma* is to be understood as this creative urge in the imperishable Reality, according to *Bhagavad-Gītā* (VIII.3), as already explained (see page 23). The cyclic process of becoming occurs incessantly and universally. Each of the minute parts of the world is subject to this process, and as a result, every existent being is in a state of constant change. But the Reality that continues to exist in and through these constantly altering states is one and the same. The continuity of change that is the world is provided for by the one Consciousness, which is also Existence. Such is the message of the *Brahma-Sūtras* passage in question and its sister passage found in *Bṛhadāraṇyaka Upaniṣad* given above.

Saṁsāra is a keyword in classical Vedānta. It is usually taken to mean the cyclic process of births and deaths that a soul undergoes. But the word literally means "becoming" or "that which constantly changes." So it is really the state or aspect of existence in constant flux.

It is not merely human beings, or the souls supposedly seated in human bodies, that are subject to this change. It is a universal process encompassing all things. The analogy of the goldsmith working a piece of gold, which comes side by side with the analogy of the caterpillar passing through blades of grass, enables us to conceive a living picture of this universal process. It is a picture in which the world's countless forms are incessantly coming and going, while the one existent Reality remains the same. As the goldsmith plies his trade, the gold assumes an ever-changing array of shapes and conditions, while always remaining the same gold. As an expression of this universal principle, this section of *Brahma-Sūtras* is known as the *tad-antara-pratipatty-adhikaraṇam* (section dealing with obtaining further stages) and it consists of seven *sūtra*s beginning with III.1.3. It does not express the idea of soul-transmigration. Instead it presents a picture of the living process of universal change, which is the beginningless and endless creativity of the ever-existent Reality.

The next section commonly held to deal with reincarnation immediately follows the section just discussed. It is titled *kr̥tatyaya-adhikaraṇam* (section dealing with *kr̥tatyaya*), and consists of *sūtra*s 8 through 11. The first *sūtra* of this section reads in the original as:

> *kr̥tatyaye 'nuśayavān dr̥ṣṭasmr̥tibhyām yathetam anevam ca.*[3]

This *sūtra* is usually interpreted by taking the imagery from *Chāndogya Upaniṣad*, quoted earlier on pages 39 above, as the authoritative guide. As such, it reads:

> On the passing away of the works (the soul re-descends) with a remainder, according to scripture and *smr̥ti*, as it went (i.e. passing through the same stations) and not thus (i.e. in the inverse order).

Here again many words and ideas are interpolated for the sake of interpretation. But when we eliminate all such interpolations and try to make direct sense of this section, we again get a different picture, which could be understood as this:

> The one eternal Reality appears here in the manifest form of the ever-changing world. Countless are the individual forms that emerge and merge again as part of this creative changefulness. Even a grain of sand is part of this eternal becoming and participates in its eternal flow. Everything within this flow is always in the process of changing from one state to another. Every such change is an event involving some kind of activity. It forms part of the total

3 *Brahma-Sūtras* III.i.8.

> creativity of the one Existent Reality; and that creativity is known as *karma*. This *karma* does not belong to an individual. Every change is merely the creative self-unfoldment of one eternal Reality. (Our words.)

So all *karmas* form one *karma* that belongs to the one Reality alone. We can learn to see the very same Reality as appearing in the form of all our activities and functions. With humans, activities and functions manifest either through volition or automatically. In either case, the individual does not ultimately create, decide or dictate his ability to function or act in a particular way. It is the total Nature that functions in the form of the particular individual, with personal characteristics and free will. Thus, everything done by the individual should be understood as part of the total *karma* of the total Nature. An individual, truly with such an understanding, cannot act with a sense of agency (*kartṛtva*). He will be fully aware that he is doing all actions as part of the total flow of *karma*.

The human can only find stability, peace and happiness in life by realizing his or her oneness with the totality in all respects. As such, one will play one's part without a sense of agency or benefit-motive. One will enjoy what comes to one by chance as part of the total flow of *karma*. This is the meaning of *karma-yoga* in *Bhagavad-Gītā*. Introducing this way of looking at one's activities, Kṛṣṇa tells Arjuna:

> Your concern should be with action as such alone, not for any benefit ever. Do not become benefit motivated; be not attached to inaction either.[4]

In another context, Kṛṣṇa tells Arjuna:

> Therefore at all times remember Me and fight.[5]

---

4 *Bhagavad-Gītā* II.47.

5 Ibid. VIII.7.

Kṛṣṇa here stands for the absolute Reality. His words mean that Arjuna should fight with the understanding or perception that *Brahman* is the only Reality; that everything that happens here is merely an aspect of the creative self-unfoldment of *Brahman*; and that his act of fighting is merely a minute part of that vast *karma*. On remembering this, Arjuna would not have any sense of agency or doership in his act of fighting. In the absence of *kartṛtva*, there will be no motive for a particular benefit either. There can be neither sense of agency nor sense of benefit motive when *karma* is understood rightly.

The characteristic forms that something will assume, or the peculiar changes it will go through, depend upon the unique nature of the forms and changes that preceded it. Such changes in the total *prakṛti* are unpredictable. That is why the future is so unpredictable. When an event occurs at a given point or moment prior to another, it is designated a cause by us; and the subsequent event or state of existence is designated its effect. This is how cause and effect are to be understood as related. According to modern science, something is considered to be understood when it is shown to be the effect of some related cause. But no scientist or philosopher can predict exactly how a current event will cause the outcome of a later event. They can only calculate certain probabilities, and they are honest enough to admit this. For this reason, none predicts with certainty the future condition of either the world or the individual. It then goes without saying that it is impossible for science to predict our future or the "hereafter" with any reasonable degree of certitude. Instead, we can only admit the great Mystery that life is, since we can neither employ reason nor the law of causality to predict what is well beyond our purview. We can only say that each of us, along with our reasoning power, is merely a spark of that great self-unfolding Mystery.

Only such awareness makes life well founded and peaceful, without room for doubt. One who is thus well founded will no longer be curious about death or life after death. Instead, his only aspiration will be to live as part of this great Mystery and experience the meaning of life itself as this Mystery.

Karma related to the emergence and re-mergence of all beings, called birth and death, also takes place within this great Mystery. The nature of any action occurring at a given moment depends on the nature of the actions preceding it. Therefore the nature of any newly-emerging form is pendent upon what has happened prior to its emergence. This is so even for the tiniest event or form that appears within Nature's overall kārmic flow. In this sense alone can we say that *karma* related to an individual being, at a given moment or state of existence, will decide the nature of a newly-emerging form and its subsequent *karma*s. In other words, everything done by an individual, which is really part of the overall flow of *karma*, ends up also being an *anuśaya*. The word *anuśaya* literally means "that which lies in continuation." In this context, we could use *anuśaya* in the sense that everything done has the potential for a consequent event, or the emergence of a new form. Each *karma* done through an individual is thus an *anuśayavān* (possessor of the potential for a new emergence), and that is part of the total *karma*. This is the nature of *karma* presented by the Upaniṣads. It can be seen in the above *sūtra* and within the overall context of *Chāndogya Upaniṣad*.

Birth Determined by Karma

The belief that a being's past *karma* determines its future form of birth is deeply rooted in all religious traditions of Indian origin. This belief needn't be rejected as meaningless. There is a sense in which it can be cogently understood and accepted even today.

We have noticed that *karma* does not belong to any individual. *Karma* is the creative urge in Reality as a whole. This *karma* becomes manifest in the form of the eternal flow of events. The inner urge in an individual human to know (*jñāna-śakti*), will (*icchā-śakti*) and act (*kriyā-śakti*) forms part of this manifestation. The nature of one event in this total event flow depends on events immediately preceding it; and this chain of sequential actions continues endlessly. As the result of every event, some change occurs. Where there is change, an older state ends with the emergence of a new one. That means, the nature of a newborn state or being depends on what happened prior to its emergence. To get a clearer idea, we can watch a sequence of breakers emerging and re-merging upon the seashore, one after another. Notice that the size, shape and force of one breaker helps determine the size, shape and force of the next. Likewise, because everything is changeful in this world, everything is intimately connected with the change of something else.

Human life is also ruled by the same phenomena. A person's thinking patterns, activities and overall lifestyle influence people. The range and extent of this influence depends on how universal their value is. Such an influence carries not only to those in proximity but also to future generations. This means that everyone's personal characteristics are decided, to an extent, by the characteristics of their predecessors. Similarly, the peculiarities of one generation depend to an extent on those of the preceding generations. We see this principle to even form the basis of modern genetics. All the information in regard to bodily features and even one's capabilities to move, think and live are encoded in one's genes. The combination of such information in a gene alters constantly due to mutation, selection and chance. Such genes are transmitted from both parents to their offspring. A new person is thus born with certain distinct characteristics. Recent genetic research is discovering that genes are more plastic than once understood. As a person acquires knowledge and experience, performing deeds in his own characteristic way, new additions and combinations may possibly be added into the gene code. Such alterations are then genetically transmitted unto the next generation in a consistent and constant process of generational transmission. Thus, in this sense, it is correct to say that every newborn being's nature depends upon the nature of *karma* that preceded it.

It would not be out of place to imagine that the genetic process was envisioned by the ancient Indian *ṛṣis* in their own peculiar way, during a time when modern genetics and scientific methods of enquiry were quite unknown. The theory of reincarnation encompasses the belief that *karma*s of a person's life are carried into the next life. The genes that parents transmit to their offspring may also contain the essence of their *karma*s (actions done mentally, verbally and physically). Thus there is only one basic difference between the theories of kārmic reincarnation and of modern genetics. The theory of kārmic reincarnation presupposes that a particular person has a soul, which leaves the body at death along with its accumulated *karma*s, and then takes a new birth by entering a new mother's womb. Such an idea has no place in genetics or science. But should we fight shy of the soul, as a general rule, in all our scientific thinking? This seems to be a problem that must be seriously considered by scientists of the future.

From the Advaitin's viewpoint, *Ātmā* is only one in number, and Its oneness is not affected by the apparent multiplicity of bodies. As such, there is only one Self that enters all the wombs, so to speak. These wombs are also nothing but the very same Self become manifest in a variant way. In his written works, Narayana Guru also underscores the oneness of the Self. Hence, the difference found between the Indian religious believers and modern geneticists is perhaps not so significant. In one work, Narayana Guru depicts the life of an individual being as comparable to a two-tiered oil lamp that constantly revolves and hanging at the middle of a beginningless and endless chain. This chain stands for the eternality of life as a universal phenomenon. This lamp has five petals in each of its two tiers. These petals represent the senses and their objects. The flickering flames, which stand for the various ways in which knowledge becomes manifest, have mental faculties for their wicks and hereditary latent memories (*vāsanās*) for oil.[6]

Viewed religiously, philosophically or scientifically, *karma*s are thus prolonged, forming a beginningless and endless chain. The problem becomes somewhat obscured when the idea of a soul's transmigration from one body unto another comes between these two aspects of *karma*. This idea has its origin in the concept that body and soul are two distinct entities. But no one has ever experienced one's own existence as a soul without a body or as a body without a soul. The duality between body and soul is merely conceptual. In other words, it only exists in our minds. In actuality, body and soul exist nowhere in our experience as two. Scientists and philosophers themselves often profess the oneness of Reality.

So dividing Reality into body and mind, and then taking Reality to be a combination of these two is itself the fundamental error underlying the body–soul problem. Body and soul are not actual entities. What can be taken as actual is the living being. But the living being can be viewed from two perspectives: in one, the body, it appears gross in nature; in the other, the soul, it seems intangible and elusive. Body and soul exist and differ as concepts. But our self-existence is what we experience actually and directly; this experience of self-existence precedes the bifurcated concepts of body and soul. Yet the possibility of this unitary and indivisible neutral Reality appearing in two mutually exclusive forms or conceptual aspects exists. The origin and resolution of this duality, like all senses of duality, is not logically explainable. We can only say that it is part of Reality's mystery. Likewise, life as a whole cannot be understood by logic alone. The blind belief that logic can explain life in its entirety is why many such mysteries puzzle us. Such is the fundamental nature

6 See Narayana Guru's *Ātmopadeśa-Śatakam* v. 17.

of error that the human mind confronts. Rather, logic itself can be seen as but one of the numerous manifestations in which Reality or Consciousness finds self-expression.

The nature of this error, and how to correct it, is revealed by Narayana Guru in his *Ātmopadeśa-Śatakam* as follows:

> Countless particles of dust constitute earth;
> And without separate being,
> Earth exists throughout those particles.
> Likewise, matter abides in mind,
> And mind in the material body.
> The two thus become revealed as one,
> When contemplatively perceived.[7]

The earth upon which we stand is an entity. It is constituted of small particles. What we call earth is merely a conglomeration of particles. A question can then arise: does the earth exist in the particles or vice versa? It can be answered both ways. Or, it could be said there is no proper answer to this question. The truth is that it is not a case of one existing in the other. One and the same reality, when looked at as a whole, is called earth; and when looked at from the perspective of constituent elements it is called particles. The earth and the particles do not exist differently as entities. We have merely created two ideas about one non-dual entity by observing it from two different angles. Treating these two ideas as two different entities is a mistake. The question, which exists in which, arises out of this mistake. Thus the question is basically wrong and therefore it has no proper answer. The same is the case of the body–soul or mind–matter duality.

We are neither aware of a body nor a soul in the direct experience of our existence. But on having this experience our intellect analyses it in order to find out its constituent elements, and finally we conclude that there is a body and an animating

7 See Narayana Guru's *Ātmopadeśa-Śatakam* v. 17.

principle called the soul. The analogy of a machine makes it easy to understand, but we forget that we do not live and think like machines. The idea of mind and body as the constituent elements of our existence is merely an artefact of our intellect. Even when we conceive of the idea of the duality, the actual experience of our existence continues to remain a unity. The answer to whether the body abides in mind or the mind abides in body has been searched for probably since man began to think. A reasonable answer has not so far been found. It is merely because the question is wrong. Even the intellect, which bifurcates our existence into mind on the one side and body on the other, has its existence as a spark within the unfathomable blaze of Reality. The capability of the thinking intellect is but a speck of the vast creative urge (*karma*) within the ultimate Reality. We may mistakenly think we can measure that Reality with such an intelligence. This kind of attempt to measure It will take us nowhere near the ineffable totality of that Reality.

Good and Evil Actions

The section known as Kr̥tatyaya Adhikaraṇam of *Brahma-Sūtras* ends with the *sūtra*:

> But (*caraṇa* means) nothing but good and evil work; thus opines Bādari.[8]

Nature's flow is also the flow of actions. Are these actions good or evil? Every action can be considered good when seen as part of the Nature's total flow or as an aspect of the Self's expression. That is why *Taittirīya Upaniṣad* (II.7.1) states that whatever emerges from the causal Reality is well made or well done (*sukr̥ta*). The word *sukr̥ta* also means "meritorious deeds". There is nothing that does not form part of this *sukr̥ta*. Even a grain of sand has a part and role in the cosmic system. Humankind alone might worry over the good or evil of their actions. This is so because humans

8 *Brahma-Sūtras* III.i.11.

can exercise free will over what they do. All other beings participate in Nature's flow without free will. Humans alone have free will and exercise it as if compelled by the inevitability of Nature. This offers humans the opportunity to doubt the propriety of their actions and feel responsible for them. Thus humans may think they will have to enjoy or suffer the results of their actions. This makes them conscious of sin and merit, and also binds them to their actions. This bondage is known as *karma-bandha*. Because of the free will in actions, and the consequences they are affixed on, humans usually remain oblivious to the fact that their being is but a part of the Nature *in toto*. What we call Nature is in turn nothing but the creative urge of one Reality or Self. Those who know this do not worry about the sinfulness, or otherwise, in what they do; they know all functions of Nature are *sukr̥ta*. The human thus finds him free from sin and merit. It is this absolutist stand that the Upaniṣads hold highest.

> Verily, such a one is not tormented by the thoughts,
> "Why have I not done right?
> Why have I done the sinful?"
> He who knows thus saves himself from these thoughts.
> For truly from both these he saves himself.[9]

Those who are not aware of the Self Reality, with Its self creativity, take upon themselves the agency of actions, which really belongs to Nature. As such, the load becomes too heavy for these ignorant ones. In an absolutist sense, only actions viewed thus are to be considered "sinful."

The next section following Kr̥tatyaya Adhikaraṇam of *Brahma-Sūtras* is Aniṣṭhādhikārī Adhikaraṇam. This section is commonly interpreted to mean that those who do not perform rituals go directly after death to *sāmyamana* (the underworld) instead of going to the sun or moon worlds. All claims made in the *sūtras* will always have some Upaniṣadic statement as their basis. This

---

9 *Taittirīya Upaniṣad* II.ix.1.

section is supposedly based on stanza II.6 of *Kaṭha Upaniṣad*, which reads as follows:

> What lies beyond shines not to the simple minded, careless, who is deluded by the glamour of wealth. Thinking, this world exists and there is no other, he falls again and again into my power.[10]

These are the words of Death (Yama). When Death says, "he falls again and again into my power," what is meant is that such a person attains death again and again. Naturally, there should be birth again and again in order that there be death again and again. It is evident from the stanza previous to this one that this statement concerns those abiding in the midst of *avidyā*. The previous stanza reads as follows:

> Abiding in the midst of ignorance, wise in their own esteem, thinking themselves to be learned, fools treading a tortuous path, go about like blind men led by one himself who is blind.[11]

So it is only such ignorant people who go to death again and again, as stated in the above verses. The verse in question then is meant to describe ignorant persons' understanding of their own life, rather than describing the essential teaching of the Upaniṣad. Death is considered a reality by the ignorant. Birth also then becomes a reality, as does the repetition of births. Even when explaining that the wrong idea of reality leads one unto death again and again, the Upaniṣad mentions nothing about *sāmyamana*.

To be precise, birth, death and rebirth are seen to be real only by those who live in the world of *avidyā* or *māyā*. Such phenomena are mere illusory appearances according to basic tenets of Vedānta. No Vedāntin will consider the effects of *māyā* to form part of the doctrine taught by any Upaniṣad. All Upaniṣads aim to teach the oneness of Reality, which has no

---

10 *Kaṭha Upaniṣad* II.6.

11 Ibid. II.5.

birth or death, and which is beyond all multiplicity. The very next stanza of *Kaṭha Upaniṣad* emphasizes the ultimate teaching by saying:

> He who cannot even be heard of by many, whom most, even on hearing, do not know, wondrous is he who can teach (Him), and skilful is he who finds (Him), and wondrous is he who knows, instructed by the wise.[12]

The previous two stanzas evidently serve the purpose of contrasting the deluded understanding of the ignorant with the real doctrine taught in the present verse.

Strictly speaking, according to the Advaitin, reincarnation, if there is any, is part of the effect of *māyā*. It is relevant only when one is subject to *avidyā*. It is never relevant in the context of the ultimate Reality sought by a Vedāntin. The question of reincarnation becomes meaningful only where the multiplicity of souls, with their births and deaths, are considered real; that is to say, when one is subject to *avidyā*. Vedānta's final teaching is that the multiplicity of souls and everything else is but an illusory appearance. For this reason, reincarnation is not a topic of serious consideration in Vedāntic thought, at least according to the Advaita School.

What is assumed real, because of the delusion caused by *māyā*, is really unreal. There is no need of a scripture or science to teach what is unreal. Scriptures as well as science try to help us arrive at a certainty about what is real. But in determining what is real, it may be necessary to state what is unreal in contrast to the real, so as to eliminate superfluous assumptions. Any deliberation upon what is to be eliminated will never form part of a scripture's ultimate teaching. Śaṅkara also discusses the topic of reincarnation, but only after making it clear that birth and death are assumed to be real because of *māyā*. Hence it is not intended

---

12 *Kaṭha Upaniṣad* II.7.

to be taken as the doctrine of Reality taught by the Upaniṣads or Śaṅkara himself. So the propriety of the statements in Aniṣṭhādhikārī Adhikaraṇam seems questionable if they are understood to have *Kaṭha Upaniṣad* passages above as their basis.

Narayana Guru in his *Ātmopadeśa-Śatakam*, as asserted by *Kaṭha Upaniṣad* (II.18) and *Bhagavad-Gītā* (II.20), reiterates the basic tenet that the ultimate Reality is never born and never dies:

> There is no death or birth nor duration of life;
> Neither man, gods nor other beings,
> being mere names and forms;
> What seems to exist is a phenomenon resembling
> the water of a mirage,
> It has no existence; be aware![13]

Besides, Narayana Guru asserts categorically in the very next verse that what we call birth and death are merely aspects of the eternal flux of becoming of the one Consciousness. In Narayana Guru's own words:

> At the time of birth there can be no existence,
> And the one who is born cannot be at another
> moment either;
> How can it ever have an existence?
> Death too is likewise; and birth too is nought.
> All is merely a flux of becoming of the pure
> Consciousness.[14]

The one who is born cannot exist at the time of birth. If he exists, then there is no need of birth. The one who is born does not exist at another moment either, because one is only a born being at the time of birth. The one who is born thus does not exist at the time of birth or at any time. Birth and death are therefore unreal. What is real is the one Consciousness or *Ātman* alone whose flux of

---

13 Narayana Guru, *Ātmopadeśa-Śatakam* v. 78.

14 Ibid. v. 79.

becoming appears as everything. Such is the contention of the Guru in this verse. Here he neither relies on scriptural evidence nor anyone's direct experience to conclude that what we call birth and death are unreal. Instead he takes to simple logic.

Looked at from the side of bodily existence, Narayana Guru says:

> To break up, to stay on and to change over again
> Is the inherent nature of the body.[15]

This bodily changefulness continues incessantly, but it does not affect the changelessness of the one Substance or Reality. When looked at from the side of the ultimate Reality, Narayana Guru says:

> The Self witnesses these three from on high;
> The cleftless one — it ever remains changeless.[16]

In other words, the Self is the Substance that provides for all the changefulness of becoming while remaining the changeless witness of these changes. It is the changeless and the indivisible Reality.

When the multifariousness of the becoming-flux, consisting of birth, life-duration and death, is understood as merely the superimposed forms upon the changeless reality of the Self, there awakens an awareness in which the momentary appearances and the eternal Reality become non-different; just as an ornament and gold are not really two entities. Narayana Guru reveals the secret of this unitive awareness in the following words:

> No one remains in this world free from the creative becoming;
> In a state of changelessness, all this is but a beginningless sport;
> On knowing the whole in its incessant continuity;
> One has unbounded happiness.[17]

---

15 Narayana Guru, *Ātmopadeśa-Śatakam* v. 83.

16 Ibid.

17 Ibid. v. 71.

That is to say, everything in the world constantly changes into ever new forms or states of existence. Nothing remains changeless. This is but mere sport going on without beginning or end. Knowing the sport in its entirety as but changefulness appearing on the changeless Reality, one attains boundless Happiness, life's ultimate consummation. Birth, death and rebirth appear real when apparent changeful forms are taken to be different from the one Reality. This sense of difference is called *dvaita* (duality) in Vedānta. One who is liberated from this sense does not return to the world of duality again, where birth and death seemed real. He sees all multiplicity as variegated changeful forms in which one and the same Reality becomes manifest. Narayana Guru enunciates this secret in the last verse of his *Darśana-Mālā* as follows:

> The one *Brahman* alone is without a second,
> Doubtlessly nothing else exists;
> Thus the knower should liberate himself from duality;
> Never again does he return.[18]

Even this verse could be easily misinterpreted by taking it to mean that the one who attains this Wisdom will not return to this world after death. Such interpretations only arise by the superimposition of the interpreter's own preconceived notions on to the text. As such, no justice is given to the author, whose implication is that the knower of *Brahman* does not return to the world of duality where birth and death appear meaningful. This verse is in conformity with a dictum given in *Gītā*, "The knower of *Brahman* finds himself in *Brahman*";[19] which is a reiteration of a passage in *Dhyānabindu Upaniṣad*.[20] Similarly the Upaniṣadic passages such as "for them there is no more returning",[21] and

18 Narayana Guru, *Darśana-Mālā* X.10.

19 *Bhagavad-Gītā* V.20.

20 *Dhyānabindu Upaniṣad* 16.

21 *Bṛhadāraṇyaka Upaniṣad* VI.ii.15.

"the liberation that is devoid of returning again",[22] are also misinterpreted to refer to a liberated man's state after death.

As we know, the nature of one's rebirth, according to the traditional theory of reincarnation, is determined by the *karma* of each individual. These *karma*s are categorized into three groups, namely *sañcita karma* (*karma*s accumulated from the past), *āgāmī karma* (impending *karma*s of the future) and *prārabdha-karma* (*karma*s already begun). We have already noted that, in strict accordance with Vedānta, *karma* is not considered as belonging to any individual, but to the total Reality. That means, to claim that an individual possesses his own *karma*s is simply due to *avidyā* (ignorance or wrong-knowing) and this is against Vedānta's teaching. If an individual possesses no *karma* whatsoever of his own, how can there be *sañcita karma, āgāmī karma* and *prārabdha karma*? Even the soul, to which *karma*s supposedly cling, is merely a superimposition caused by *avidyā*. One Reality alone exists; and It is *sat–cit–ānanda*. Even *karma* itself depends on That. A person should be aware that his existence does not differ from this one Existence. Such is the final teaching of Vedānta, and it is confirmed by Narayana Guru in the concluding verse of his *Brahmavidyā-Pañcakam* (Five Verses on the Science of *Brahman*). He says:

> Where are *sañcita, āgāmī* and *prārabdha karmas* for you,
> When *karma* itself is non-existent?
> These are but superimposed conditionings upon thy Self;
> Thou art the one Existing Consciousness,
> The all-pervading.[23]

---

22 *Mukti Upaniṣad* I.20.

23 Narayana Guru, *Brahmavidyā-Pañcakam.,* v. 5.

9

Conclusion

THERE is only one Reality. It is imperishable. It creatively transforms Itself. The creative urge in Reality, which causes the constant emergence of new forms, is called *karma*. Thus, *karma* really belongs to no individual. Manifested forms emerge and re-merge incessantly as a result of this creative urge. The emergence of a new form, in effect, is the disappearance of an old one. We call the former birth and the latter death. But the imperishable Reality continues to exist in and through all these various transformations, just as gold continues to exist in and through the various ornamental forms into which it is shaped.

This is the ultimate Reality concerning life. Those who know this Reality are called *jñānīs*. They do not see themselves as different from the imperishable Reality that was never born and will never die. They live with the awareness, "I am that Reality which was never born and will never die". The problem "what will happen after death?" does not occur to them.

Others are unaware of the ultimate Reality. They are called *ajñānīs*. They take the ever-changing appearances for reality. Each manifested form in that apparent world emerges and disappears. The ignorant naturally takes the former as birth and the latter as death. So the question "what will happen after death?" always puzzles them.

Those who are incapable of knowing Reality, taking the unreal to be the real, go on inquiring what happens after death. To pacify them, *ṛṣis* of India answered this question in a way that could be understood by those who are only aware of the world of the unreal. So the stories in the scriptures concerning life after death should be taken as pertaining to the world of the unreal. None forms a part of the scriptures' teaching proper.

Taking the unreal as real, and then trying to understand life, is known as *avidyā* in Vedānta. Birth, death, life after death and the two paths that souls supposedly take after death — all these belong to the realm of *avidyā*.

Scriptures are not meant to teach *avidyā*. Their ultimate goal is to teach *vidyā* (wisdom). The part of a scripture that forms its wisdom teaching proper should alone be treated as its teaching or doctrine.

An ignorant person can only conceive wrong ideas in regard to the fundamental truth of his own life. Yet such wrong ideation will not change what is really true concerning him. The ultimate Reality is the same, both for a *jñānī* and an *ajñānī*. But the difference is that the *jñānī* alone knows this Reality and lives accordingly, whereas the *ajñānī* mistakes something else to be real and lives in total confusion. An *ajñānī*'s ignorance makes his life full of misery and problems. The fear of life after death is but one such conundrum.

Both *jñānī* and *ajñānī* emerged as individual beings from the same imperishable Reality. They inevitably must go back to It. Not knowing this simple truth, the *ajñānī* worries over his state after death. He also does not know that *karma* really belongs to Nature and not to any particular individual. A sense of agency as well as a guilty conscience about having done evil deeds makes him all the more worried. He feels the responsibility of eating the bitter fruits of his own supposed actions either in this life or in the next, according to his belief. Great teachers used this belief to emphasize their moral instruction. They taught that those who do meritorious deeds would reap the fruits of a better life in the next birth, which might ultimately lead to final release. This teaching prompts the ignorant to lead a virtuous life in this world. It also has the added value of giving the hope of attaining immortality for men who are helplessly struggling in a world of ignorance.

As for the operation of *karma,* the nature of each new facet that emerges from the one imperishable Reality is unpredictable. Yet the nature of each such facet depends on the nature of the one just preceding it. Each facet and its peculiarities come into being as a result of the creative unfoldment (*prakṛti*) incessantly taking place. *Karma,* inherent in each facet of the whole, apparently determines the inherent nature of the following facet yet to emerge. In this limited sense it would not be wrong to say that *karma* of one individual decides the nature of the next being to emerge.

To summarize, for a *jñānī,* there is neither birth nor death nor reincarnation. For an *ajñānī,* birth, death and rebirth appear real. So one can decide this matter with a view proper to oneself. None the less, Reality always remains the same, regardless of whether or not we change our viewpoint. Whether known or not, Reality always remains Reality — *sat, cit* and *ānanda.*

Glossary

Adhyātma : Loosely translated as spirituality. Strictly, that kind of knowledge which tries to understand everything with one's self-existence as the point of reference (from *adhi* = to make a basis, and *ātma* = oneself or the self).

Āgāmī Karma : See *Karma.*

Ajñānin (ajñānī) : The ignorant. The opposite *of jñānin (jñānī).*

Akṣara Puruṣa : The imperishable person. The personified concept of *Brahman.*

Ānanda : Bliss to be understood in the context of the Good in Western philosophy as a Supreme Value. *Sat, cit* and *ānanda* are terms conjointly used to describe the Absolute (*Brahman*) in Vedānta. Related to an individual, it is the value consciousness that enables one to evaluate one's own experience either as pleasant or unpleasant.

Aparā : See *parā.*

Ātman (ātmā) : The self (from the root *āp* = to pervade). The invisible reality or stuff that pervades any visible form. Often confused with *jīva* (the soul). Used in slightly altered senses according to contexts. The simplest meaning of the word is "I" or "oneself."

Ātmopadeśa-Śatakam : One of the major philosophical com-positions of

Nārāyaṇa Guru in the Malayalam language, of one hundred verses. Literally, "One Hundred Verses of Self-Instruction."

Avidyā : Nescience, ignorance. Equivalent, of *māyā*, darkness and the opposite of *vidyā*. The function of consciousness that causes taking the unreal as the real and the real as unreal.

Bhagavad-Gītā : Part of *Mahābhārata* (an epic of India) consisting of eighteen chapters, in which Kṛṣṇa as *guru* instructs Arjuna the secrets of the mysterious science of contemplation called *Brahma-vidyā* or Yoga Śāstra. It contains the quintessence of all the Upaniṣads.

Brahman : The Absolute. Literally that which is always growing. The Vedāntic word for God, which is neither a He nor a She nor even a person.

Brahma-vidyā : The science of *Brahman* or the Absolute. Another name of Vedānta.

Cāṇḍāla : A general name for the lowest caste or the outcaste, not belonging to any of the four castes of the caste system of India.

Cit : Literally, consciousness. The all-pervading imperishable Reality in all the perishable apparent forms is invisible and its is pure Consciousness in essence. Hence *Brahman* is designated as *cit*. See *sat* and *ānanda* also.

Darśana-Mālā : One of the major philosophical com-positions of Narayana Guru in the Sanskrit language. Literally, "The Garland of Visions". It consists of ten chapters of ten verses each. Each chapter is a vision of the Absolute from a particular philosophical perspective. All the ten visions are strung together in the invisible thread of Advaita or non-duality.

Deha : The physical body. Literally, that which could be anointed.

Dehī (dehīn) : The substance that assumes a visible form or body. See *deha*.

Devatā : A deity. A god as understood in the context of adoration or worship. Every Vedic hymn has a deity who is praised, a *chanda*s (a particular metre in which it is composed), and an *ṛṣi*, the seer who composed it.

Deva-yāna : The path of the gods. One of the two paths through which the departed souls supposedly go to the other world from where they will not return. Literally, the bright path. Also called *śukla-gati*, the white path and *arcir-mārga* (the path of brightness). See *pitṛ-yāna*.

Guṇas : Qualities or functional peculiarities inherent in nature. *Sattva, rajas* and *tamas* are the three specializing *guṇa*s found in nature.

Guru : From *gu* = darkness and *ru* = to counteract. The banisher of darkness or ignorance. A spiritual teacher or preceptor.

Icchā-śakti : The power of volition. One of the three powers of an individual. See *kriyā-śakti* and *jñāna-śakti*.

Iśvara : The Sanskrit equivalent to God. Literally, one who controls everything.

Jīva : The Sanskrit equivalent to soul. Often confused with *ātmā*, the Self.

Jñāna-śakti : The power to know. One of the three powers of an individual. See *kriyā-śakti* and *icchā-śakti.*

Jñānin (*jñānī*) : One who has attained enlightenment. *Jñāna* means wisdom as contrasted with *karma* (works). *Jñāna-mārga* (the way of wisdom) gives primacy to reason and intuition.

Karma : All actions in general. Philosophically the creative urge inherent in the Imperishable Reality, causing the emergence of all manifest forms. In the Vedic context, the ritual of burnt-sacrifice enjoined by the Vedas. As a religious belief of the Hindus, the incipient memory factors that cling to the souls as a result of their deeds. All are bound to enjoy or suffer the fruits of their deeds, and will have to reincarnate for this purpose. One might be accumulating more *karma*s in the new birth. This vicious chain of action goes on till one attains final release. Such *karma*s are divided into three categories — *sañcita karma* (the actions accumulated in all the previous births), *āgāmī karma* (fresh actions done in the present life time) and *prārabdha karma* (actions already initiated but the eating of their fruits is not finished with).

Kriyā-śakti : Power to act. One of the three powers of an individual. See *jñāna-śakti* and *icchā-śakti.*

Kṣara-puruṣa : The perishable person referring to the individual soul.

Kṣatriya : The warrior class. One of the four classes of the Indian caste system. Originally refers to the psychological type who have prowess, brightness, firmness, skill, generosity, dignity and never-absconding as their main characteristics.

Māyā : Literally, that which does not exist. Connotes a factor of epistemological and methodological importance in Śaṅkara's Vedānta especially. Whatever is postulated as the cause of the unreal spoken of, in the most generic of categorical terms in philosophy as against theology, is to be laid at the door of *māyā*. It is the basis of duality or synergic antinomies. Metaphysically, the creative potential dormant in *Brahman* for self-unfoldment as everything apparent.

Mukti : The final release. Normally refers to release that is gained after death. Philosophically the experiencing of Absolute Freedom while living. Also called *mokṣa.*

Naciketas : Youth mentioned in *Kaṭha Upaniṣad,* who has a discussion with Death who instructs him in higher Wisdom. He represents the youthful, bright, spirit of man desirous of emancipation, while his father typifies the failure and bankruptcy of life dominated by ritual and longing for heaven.

Neti neti : This refers to the method of negative reasoning which is at the basis of the Vedāntic approach to Wisdom. Literally it means "not this, not this." By the elimination of the irrelevant and extraneous factors which prevent the coming of Wisdom, illumination results automatically, without effort or action. This corresponds to the *via negativa* of the Europian mystics. The path of withdrawal (*nivṛtti mārga),* which is often opposed to the path of action (*pravṛtti mārga*), means also the same attitude of disciplined negation.

Pañcāgni-vidyā : The science of five fires. Knowledge concerning five sacrifical fires maintained by orthodox Hindus — *dakṣiṇāgni, gārhapatyāgni, āhavanīyāgni, sabhyāgni,* and *āvasathāgni.*

Parā : The beyond. Pertaining to the Ultimate or Supreme, as opposed to the immanent here and now aspect of reality, which is *aparā.*

Pitṛ-loka : The world of the departed souls. (From *pitṛ* = manes or departed souls and *loka* = the world.)

Pitṛ-yāna : The path of the manes. One of the two paths through which the departed souls are supposed to travel to the other world from where they are destined to return. Also called *kṛṣṇa-gati,* the black path *dhūma-mārga* (the path of smoke). See *deva-yāna.*

Prajāpati : Literally, the lord of those who are born. Name applied to the Creator as the progenitor or originator of all living beings, and representing an ontological version of Brahmā, the Creator.

Prakṛti : Nature. Literally, that which is always in an active state. This activeness is inherent in the ultimate Reality or *Brahman. Brahman* in an active state is called *prakṛti.*

Prāṇa : The vital breath. The functions of vital breath are classified into five — *prāṇa* (going upward), *apāna* (going downward), *vyāna* (that which takes vitality to every part of the body), *samāna* (that which keeps the balance of the body) and *udāna* (that which leaves the body at death).

Prārabdha karma : See *karma.*

Prati-prasava : From *prati* = backward and *prasava* = giving birth. According to Sāṁkhya and Yoga systems of philosophy, every individual being came into existence as a result of the evolutive process going on in Nature (*prakṛti*). This process is called *prasava*. A man, one of the beings thus born, goes backward in search of *prakṛti* or Nature from which he was born. Such a process is called *prati-prasava* in the Yoga system of Patañjali.

Purāṇa : Literally, the ancient. The collection of legends of antiquity, meant mainly for teaching ordinary people, the philosophy of the Upaniṣads with the help of numerous tales.

Puruṣa : Literally, "person." The word is used both in the universal and particular senses. In the universal sense He is the cosmic Person who has the entire cosmos for His body. In this sense He is often called *virāṭ-puruṣa*.

Puruṣottama : The Absolute Principle or Godhead as distinct from demi-urges and divinities of various religious expressions. *Puruṣa* in Sāṁkhya philosophy is the spiritual principle as contrasted with *prakṛti* or Nature. When Advaita revalues this concept of *puruṣa* in an effort to raise it above all taint of dual implications, the idea of *puruṣottama* arises, as in chapter XV of *Bhagavad-Gītā*, where there is a transcendence of both the eternal and the transient aspects of reality.

Rāmāyaṇa : An epic (like *Mahābhārata*) composed by Vālmīki centred round the history of Rāma, the king of Ayodhyā, who travelled to the extreme south of India and to Laṅkā. *Rāmāyaṇa* brings into juxtaposition the Āryan and the proto-Āryan civilizations of India.

Ṛṣi	:	Literally, a seer; a seer of the Reality. Name applied to wise sages of ancient India who lived generally in the seclusion of forests and wrote holy scriptures of canonical importance and classical value. They were not necessarily monks, and many of them had their wives living with them. *Maharṣi* means a great *ṛṣi.*
Sañcita Karma	:	See *karma.*
Śarīra	:	Literally, that which perishes. The physical body or the visible form.
Sat	:	Existence. That which exists always. The subsisting reality in all the transient forms of the visible world, just as gold is the subsisting reality in all ornaments. *Brahman* as this subsisting Reality is designated as *sat.* See *ānanda* and *cit* also.
Śruti	:	That which is heard. The words heard from a *guru.* The recorded utterings of the past *guru*s concerning pure Wisdom teachings of eternal value. All the Upaniṣads are considered śrutis.
Śukla-gati	:	See *deva-yāna.*
Sukṛta	:	Literally, well done. In the Vedic sense the meticulous performance of rituals and the merits accrued through them. Any meritorious deed. The merit achieved through such deeds. One who has done such deeds.
Sūtra	:	An aphorism. An ancient literary style in the Sanskrit language, in which extremely short sentences implicitly convey vast ideas.
Upaniṣad	:	Wisdom texts appended to Vedas. Also called Vedānta as it appears at the end of Vedas, and *jñāna-*

kāṇḍa as it deals with Wisdom. The word literally means, "to sit nearby and below" (*upa* = just below, *ni* = nearby, *ṣat* = to sit down). The name indicates a diściple sitting beside a *guru*. The word also means, "the secret teaching". Upaniṣads teach the philosophy of *Brahman*, the Absolute. The ten major Upaniṣads are *Īśa, Kena, Kaṭha, Praśna, Muṇḍaka, Māṇḍūkya, Taittirīya, Aitareya, Chāndogya* and *Bṛhadāraṇyaka*.

Vaiśya : One of the four castes of the Indian caste system — the merchant and the agriculturist class. As a psychological type, those who find life-fulfilment in farming, tending cattle and trading.

Vedas : The earliest of the Indian scriptures, collated into four volumes — *Ṛgveda, Yajurveda, Sāmaveda* and *Atharvaveda*. They praise gods like Indra, Varuṇa, Mitra and other phenomenal gods of nature. They were later overcome by the Upaniṣads. The word *veda* means knowledge. The Vedas generally stand for rituals (*karma*).

Vidyā : Knowledge. The function of conscious-ness by which one understands the real as real and the unreal as unreal.

Virāṭ-puruṣa : See *puruṣa*.

Vivekacūḍāmaṇi : "The Crest Jewel of Discrimination", an introductory textbook on Vedānta by Śaṅkara.

Vyāsa : The son of Parāśara born of a fisher-maid. Otherwise known as Veda Vyāsa. He was also the author of *Brahma-Sūtras*. Known also as Bādarāyaṇa, he is the most important of the personalities of Indian spirituality.

Yajña : A sacrifice, sacrificial rite, any offering or oblation.

Yājñavalkya : An *ṛṣi.* The most important teacher of *Bṛhadāraṇyaka Upaniṣad.*

Yoga : From the root *yuj* = to join. Psychic union of the self with the Self, just as an ornament finds its oneness with gold. As a contemplative method of expression, the way of expressing an inexpressible reality by showing its two opposite sides and leaving the unitive meaning to be grasped by the reader or seeker. For example, attaining immortality and crossing over death are two expressions meaning the same. But these two expressions are opposite in nature. They have in between them a meaning that cannot be expressed as it is. Equivalent to the Platonic method of "dialectics" of the West.

Bibliography

Bhaskaran, T., *Śreenārāyaṇa Guruvinte Sampoorṇa Kritikal* (Malayalam) (Complete Works of Śrī Nārāyaṇa Guru with commentary), Calicut: Mathrubhoomi Publications, 1985.

Briggs, John P., *Looking Class Universe,* New York: Corner Stone Library, 1984.

Capra, Fritjof, *The Tao of Physics,* Glasgow: Fantana Paperbacks, 1988.

Chakravarti, V.R. Srisaila, *The Philosophy of Sri Ramanuja,* Madras: V.R.S. Chakravarti, 1974.

Hawking, Stephen W., *A Brief History of Time,* New York: Bantam Books, 1988.

Hofstadter, Douglas R., *The Mind's I,* New York: Bantam Books, 1982.

Keith, A.B., *The Religion and Philosophy of the Veda and Upanisads,* Delhi: Motilal Banarsidass, 1970.

Narayanan Namboodiripad, O.M.C., *The Ṛg Veda* (Malayalam), Trichur: Kairali Press and Books, 1982.

Nataraja Guru, *An Integrated Science of the Absolute,* Varkala: Narayana Gurukula, 1977.

——— *The Bhagavad Gītā* — Commentary, Varkala: Narayana Gurukula, 1989.

——— *The Autobiography of an Absolutist,* Varkala, Narayana Gurukula, 1989.

——— *Life and Teachings of Narayana Guru,* Varkala: Narayana Gurukula, 1990.

——— *Dialectical Methodology,* Varkala: Narayana Gurukula, 1977.

——— *Wisdom's Frame of Reference,* Varkala: Narayana Gurukula, 1973.

——— *The Philosophy of a Guru,* Varkala: Narayana Gurukula, 1986.

Narayana Guru, *Complete Works* (Malayalam), Varkala: Sivagiri Mutt, 1990.

Nitya Chaitanya Yati, *Neither This Nor That But Aum . . . ,* Delhi: Vikas Publishing House, 1982.

——— *The Psychology of Darśanamālā,* Varkala: Narayana Gurukula, 1987.

——— *Bhagavad Gītā Swād hyayam* (Malayalam), Varkala: Narayana Gurukula, 1989.

Panikkar, Raimunds, *The Vedic Experience*, Pondicherry: All India Books, 1977.

Prakasananda, Swami, *Śrīmad Bhagavad Gītā* — Commentary (Malayalam), Trichur: Sri Ramakrishna Mutt, 1987.

Radhakrishnan, S. (tr.), *The Principal Upaniṣads*, London: George Allen and Unwin, 1953.

Ramanujacharya, *The Vedānta Sūtras* — Commentary, tr. George Thibaut, Delhi: Motilal Banarsidass, 1984.

Śaṅkarācārya, *Vedānta-Sūtras* — Commentary, tr. George Thibaut, Delhi: Motilal Banarsidass, 1973.

——— *Vivekacūḍāmaṇi*, tr. Swami Madhavananda, Calcutta: Advaita Ashram, 1970.

——— *Bṛhadāraṇyaka Upaniṣad* — Commentary, tr. Swami Madhavananda, Calcutta: Advaita Ashram, 1988.

——— *Chāndogya Upaniṣad* — Commentary, tr. Swami Gambhirananda, Calcutta: Advaita Ashram, 1987.

——— *Eight Upaniṣads* — Commentary, tr. Swami Gambhirananda, Calcutta: Advaita Ashram, 1986.

Sharma, B.N.K., *Philosophy of Śrī Madhvācārya*, Mumbai: Bharatiya Vidya Bhavan, 1962.

Sinha, Jadunath, *Indian Psychology*, Delhi: Motilal Banarsidass, 1986.

Srinivasachari, P.N., *The Philosophy of Viśiṣṭādvaita*, Madras: Adayar Library, 1970.

Upaniṣad Saṅgrahaḥ, Delhi: Motilal Banarsidass, 1980.

Vidyananda Swami, *Darśanamālā* — Commentary (Malayalam), Varkala: Sivagiri Mutt, 1976.

Zukav, Gary, *The Dancing Wu Li Masters*, Glasgow: Fantana Paperbacks, 1989.

Index